What people are saying about ...

REPLANT

"*Replant* captures in a single story what is beginning to happen in urban centers across America. Historic churches and their sacred spaces are being rescued. Fresh stories are being rewritten, and life-giving communities are springing up to carry the baton of the previous generation. Darrin and Mark have told their compelling story at an important time in history."

Mark Jobe, lead pastor of New Life Community Church in Chicago

"Satan wants gospel-proclaiming churches to fall apart and disappear. That's why it is such an enormous challenge to replant a church that is near death. But it is a battle we must be willing to wage as hundreds of millions of dollars' worth of church properties are at risk of becoming coffee houses, art galleries, and museums in the next few years. Darrin and Mark walk us through an anatomy of their church replant. It is not a journey for the faint of heart, but all of the work and anguish are worth it when a community once again has a vibrant church where lives are being changed by Christ."

Kevin Ezell, president of North American Mission Board

"Darrin has an important voice in the future of the church, and as great leaders often do, he is helping catalyze an important conversation in *Replant*."

Bob Buford, founder of Leadership Network and author of *Halftime, Finishing Well,* and *Drucker & Me*

"The church landscape is full of once great and growing churches now declining to barely survivable sizes. One option is to close and sell. Another option is to merge or replant. Most churches choose the first by default without seriously considering the second option. *Replant* is an example of *what can be* in hundreds of churches that need to choose new life over death and decline. Told by two of the key participants, it includes the realistic portrayal of the high and low moments that have now led to a vibrant urban church."

Dave Travis, CEO (Chief Encouragement
Officer) of Leadership Network

"One of the most encouraging dynamics in Kansas City over the past five years has been the birth—and rebirth—of a church, Redeemer Fellowship. This story, so fascinatingly chronicled in *Replant* by Darrin Patrick and Mark DeVine, needs to be read by the masses. I pray what has taken place through Redeemer will be replicated in thousands of churches across North America and beyond. I am grateful for Redeemer's gospel witness in the heart of Kansas City, and I'm grateful for Darrin Patrick and Mark DeVine for telling the story."

Jason K. Allen, president of Midwestern
Baptist Theological Seminary and College

"This is a really good book! The fact is I could not put it down! It is encouragement, instruction, and inspiration in one package. And it is extremely well written. Dying churches can be revived. If you have doubts, this is the book for you!"

Daniel L. Akin, president of Southeastern
Baptist Theological Seminary

"As I read Patrick and DeVine's *Replant* (a process I am now personally engaged in), the words that kept coming to mind were *courage, creativity,* and *humility.* Each of the situations they faced required courage and creativity that they displayed with remarkable giftedness. At the same time, they have the humility to confess that every situation is different and no outcome is guaranteed. We learn from their experience, but we also are forced to see the grace upon which they depended—the grace that ultimately fueled the courage, the creativity, and the humility."

Bryan Chapell, pastor of Grace Presbyterian Church and president emeritus of Covenant Seminary

"Enough of the polite and passive person! *Replant* provides an example of the return of the bold prophetic leader who calls the church back to faithfulness and fruitfulness. In a time when despair over the state of the church is easy to come by, this volume brings hope, inspiration, and practical lessons for those who desire to contribute to the renewal and revival of the church. *Replant* is an encouraging story of faithful, courageous, and creative leadership that is clearly an outworking of the gospel of grace."

The Rev. Canon Dan Alger, director of communications and equipping for Anglican 1000, Anglican Church in North America

"I have preached in over two thousand Southern Baptist churches. I have seen small and large, old and new, institutional and missional, some growing but most declining. Reading *Replant* by Darrin Patrick and Mark DeVine moved me deeply. The authors offer a compelling story—not simply a theoretical idea—with practical wisdom to help a dying church to live again. Across America too many churches are dying. Read this book and take hope; look and live!"

Alvin L. Reid, PhD, professor of evangelism and student ministry and Bailey Smith Chair of Evangelism at Southeastern Baptist Theological Seminary, and young professionals director at Richland Creek Community Church

"Books on church renewal abound; they are often filled with statistics, social analysis, and how-to techniques. This book tells the real story of a real church that went through an amazing transformation—actually a new birth—in what can only be called a surprising work of God. This is the story of a church that was willing to die in order to live again in the power of the Holy Spirit. A great story, well told, and worth sharing with others."

Timothy George, founding dean of Beeson Divinity School at Samford University and general editor of *Reformation Commentary on Scripture*

REPLANT

REPLANT

HOW A DYING CHURCH CAN **GROW** AGAIN

MARK DeVINE | DARRIN PATRICK

transforming lives together

REPLANT
Published by David C Cook
4050 Lee Vance View
Colorado Springs, CO 80918 U.S.A.

David C Cook Distribution Canada
55 Woodslee Avenue, Paris, Ontario, Canada N3L 3E5

David C Cook U.K., Kingsway Communications
Eastbourne, East Sussex BN23 6NT, England

The graphic circle C logo is a registered trademark of David C Cook.

The website addresses recommended throughout this book are offered as a
resource to you. These websites are not intended in any way to be or imply an
endorsement on the part of David C Cook, nor do we vouch for their content.

Unless otherwise noted, all Scripture quotations are taken from The Holy
Bible, English Standard Version® (ESV®), copyright © 2001 by Crossway, a
publishing ministry of Good News Publishers. Used by permission. All rights
reserved. Scripture quotations marked NIV are taken from the Holy Bible, New
International Version®, NIV®. Copyright © 1973, 2011 by Biblica, Inc™. Used by
permission of Zondervan. All rights reserved worldwide. www.zondervan.com.

LCCN 2014932854
ISBN 978-0-7814-1032-8
eISBN 978-1-4347-0753-6

© 2014 Darrin Patrick and Mark DeVine
Published in association with the literary agency of Wolgemuth & Associates, Inc.

The Team: Alex Field, John Blase, Amy Konyndyk,
Nick Lee, Tonya Osterhouse, Karen Athen
Cover Design: Nick Lee
Cover Photo: Shutterstock

Printed in the United States of America
First Edition 2014

1 2 3 4 5 6 7 8 9 10

022814

For Drew and Sam

—MARK

||||||||||||||||||||||||||||||||||||

To all the leaders who are involved in a church plant or in a church that is thinking about being replanted: Your sacrifice, faithfulness, and courage inspire me. May God get much glory through multiplying leaders just like you so that thousands of new churches can reach millions of new people.

—DARRIN

CONTENTS

FOREWORD

You may have heard of YouTube videos "going viral." Whether it's a boy biting his brother's finger or goats bleating along to Taylor Swift, some videos are just too good *not* to share.

This idea of "going viral" needs to expand beyond the realm of home videos on YouTube. For the health of the church in America, we need a number of ideas and movements to "go viral."

In underreached areas and urban centers of the country, we need a church-planting and a church-multiplication movement to "go viral." That's one of the reasons Warren Bird and I wrote *Viral Churches*.

In some communities where the Christian influence has waned, where pews stand empty and churches are in disrepair, we need a church-renewal and replanting movement to "go viral." We need churches and pastors that are passionate, proactive, and committed to doing whatever it takes to plant new churches, and replant and revitalize existing ones.

THE TASK OF REVITALIZATION IN CHURCH PLANTING

The Western world is in need of new churches. In some cases churches must multiply and plant new churches from scratch, while in other cases existing churches must and should be revitalized—in essence, they must be "replanted."

We already know it takes a brave pastor to answer the call to plant a new church and undertake the entailing unique and vital challenges. Answering such a call requires courage, vision, and total dependence upon God. The pastor/planter must often overcome cultural resistance, inadequate facilities, and the lack of an established group with whom to work.

Yet the work of revitalization is also challenging. Here the pastor is often confronted with mounting debt, falling attendance, spiritual lethargy, and long-standing turf wars that have distracted the leadership from the true work of outreach, care, and evangelism.

Both tasks require pastors with vision, steely conviction, and foremost patient reliance on God's faithfulness. But some pastors and churches are combining the ideas into one effort.

THE VISION ABOVE AND BEYOND DIVISION

It is undeniable that churches evolve over time. Over the life of a church, neighborhoods can change, leadership can expand and even fail, theological trends can take hold, unity can be lost, and splits can occur. Throughout all of this turmoil, congregations frequently become inward-focused and often obsessed with maintaining the status quo.

Well-meaning members lose sight of their role as servants and become increasingly focused on controlling the very church they are called to serve. When a serving heart is replaced by a controlling heart, division is bound to ensue. And when selfish division lies unchallenged, areas of ministry and service become turfs to be defended, and brother and sisters in Christ become opponents and obstacles to individual accomplishment.

Pastors called into this melee must have both a vision for unity and the ability to communicate that vision through the minefields of personal preference and tradition. In many cases the history of the church and its traditions provide the pastor with the very tools necessary to effect change and renewal.

THE UNLIKELY ALLIES OF TRADITION AND HISTORY

Many pastors look at the dying churches around them, beset with congregational divisions and antiquated practices, and see nothing but problems. They see their congregation's often-rocky history and church's long-standing traditions as chains that bind the congregation and prevent renewal.

But replanting requires pastoral vision that can see beyond all that to recognize that history and tradition can be allies in forging a path toward revitalization. Many times these churches have a valuable gospel DNA; a theological tradition, lost, that needs to be recovered; and a history of God's faithfulness that needs to be retold.

The very buildings they occupy, while often outdated and in need of repair, speak to decades of faithful stewardship on the part of past congregations. Focusing on that heritage can turn history into an asset and tradition into an argument for change.

THE INTERSECTION OF MULTIPLICATION AND RENEWAL: EVANGELISM

The mission of God is more than church planting, but I think church planting and multiplication should be part of every church's mission statement. The mission of God is also more than replanting existing churches, but saving churches from death and decline must be of value to pastors who are passionate about bringing the gospel to communities in need. What unites these two paths of planting is the mission of evangelism.

Evangelism—declaring the saving gospel of Christ—is and should be the driving force of every Christian and the engine of church growth and church renewal.

Both traditional church multiplication and church replanting are motivated by evangelism.

Evangelism is an important part of the newly planted church's mission, and it is essential for the revitalization of established but faded churches in need of renewal. The passion for outreach and a practice of evangelism run like an artery, providing the lifeblood for church multiplication and church renewal.

So is there a way to unite the interests of churches looking to plant and churches in need of replanting and renewal? I would argue that there is a way.

Churches looking to multiply and plant are in need of additional space and footholds in new communities. Churches and pastors seeking renewal and looking to replant are often in need of resources and a new influx of gospel-centered individuals and vision. *Replant* provides us with the opportunity to see the firsthand account of this intersection of multiplication and renewal.

If churches are going to multiply and share the gospel of Jesus Christ throughout their communities and around the world, they must have a passion for evangelism and a true love for both planting new churches and replanting established churches in need of renewal. Evangelism is the catalyst for church multiplication and the renewal of the body of Christ worldwide.

Ed Stetzer and the LifeWay Research team

INTRODUCTION

The chain of events you are about to read actually happened in a specific time and a specific place. God brought together three unlikely men living in three different cities to redeem a distressed congregation with a magnificent building in a strategic part of an important city.

Though some unique things happened, we contend that this story is the story of many churches, denominations, pastors, and church planters.

It's a story of the providence of God, who ordered circumstances and moved the hearts of two churches and three pastors. It's a story of perseverance. Many faithful saints had served and sacrificed for 160 years to make such a story of a congregational redemption possible. It's a story of humility. A small group of people meeting in a large building with an interim pastor made the bold decision that their legacy would not be their history. It's a story of hope that dispels the myth that generations can't worship together, that established churches and new churches can't minister together.

In this story you will meet a seminary professor by day and interim pastor by night: a Southern redhead named Mark. He is the primary storyteller of this book. His bold decision to stand against complacency and evil made a dynamic kingdom partnership possible. You'll meet Kevin, the reluctant church planter who originally said no to a beautiful but worn-out building because he worried it would distract his new church from ministry. You'll meet me, Darrin. Along with the elders of The Journey, I agreed to take responsibility for a church and a building 250 miles away from me so that the gospel could go forward. I'll be extracting principles throughout to give you ideas on how to apply this in your situation. You'll see those in boxes scattered throughout the text. I also wrote the final two chapters of the book, which describe the crescendo of what God did in an unlikely situation with three radically different leaders.

This book tells a true story about something that is happening culturally in many of our cities and communities. It reveals a possible strategy for older churches and new churches to work together for greater gospel impact.

This isn't a how-to book describing four easy steps to help churches merge for more fruitfulness.[1] However, principles will emerge from the story that will aid you in similar circumstances. We hope to inspire you to take risks for God's glory, to raise your gaze to what is possible, to challenge what is comfortable, so that God's plan A—the local church—advances.

Chapter One

THE MAKING OF
A MADMAN

Between grief and nothing, I will take grief.

William Faulkner

It took me (Mark) between forty-two and forty-four years to go crazy. That's how long I had been sucking in oxygen on this earth when I began to flirt with almost certain disaster—not only voluntarily but with aforethought and calculation. I started entertaining the notion of trying to provoke an old, dying congregation in the inner city to wake up and welcome radical change even if that change threatened to kill them in the process.

Some would say my insanity commenced much earlier. They can point to official documents to prove it. My own father, in cahoots with a South Carolina psychiatrist, in the wake of a drug-induced psychotic episode, had me committed to an asylum in the spring of 1977. By 1999, having turned my back first on intravenous drug use and then on a career in electrical engineering, I willingly sold most of my earthly possessions and packed my wife and two small children into a jet headed for Thailand, so I could squat in the searing heat of a dead-end Bangkok street (*soi*) every day, amid a sea of dog excrement, in an attempt to share the gospel, in the native Thai, with a bunch of Buddhists. Both episodes expose a periodic predilection for risk taking—risk in pursuit of hallucinogenic escape from the uncertainties and assaults and fears of earthly existence in the first episode; risk in pursuit of souls on the front lines of long-tempered and largely successful Buddhist rejection of the gospel of Jesus Christ in the second. Nevertheless, informed human calculus would set the prospects for success much higher in both the psych ward and the Thai *soi* than at the intersection of 39th Street and Baltimore Avenue in midtown Kansas City, Missouri.

What prepares a man to imagine that he can stroll into an old, proud, dying city church in the Midwest and have his way with it? What allows a man to suppose he can wrench the levers of power out of the hands of a small but entrenched and fierce pack of lay Christians habituated to having their way—to imagine he can do so despite decades of failed attempts at pastoral leadership? Especially a man as ill equipped as me.

A handful of cousins and I were the first in my family to venture off of our Southern homesteads and away from our blue-collar lives to those suspicious institutions called colleges and universities. The BS, MDiv., and PhD left me a bit more presentable to polite company but failed to properly rein in my native speech.

Yet here I was, unreconstructed Southern accent and all. From the perspective of those who raised me—and even more of those who raised them—Kansas City might as well be in Canada or on the moon. Anything north of Knoxville exposed one to an array of unsavory foreign experiences: Yankees, ice, tundra, unsweetened tea, okra prepared without the benefit of an iron skillet. Yet here I was, and in spite of everything, God was about to do a wonderful work—about to draw a straight line with a crooked stick.

TWO LITTLE BOATS PASSING

You can fool some of the people some of the time, and by the spring of 1994, I managed to get myself hired to teach theology at Midwestern Baptist Theological Seminary. My original title proves that the administration and trustees of the institution retained a fair measure of prudence in my hiring. I was launched into my full-time academic career as "Visiting" Professor of Systematic Theology. In my case "visiting" did not indicate the wooing of a famous scholar to teach a course or two at Midwestern and thus adorn the faculty. No, "visiting" meant, "Don't you sit all the way down in that chair, young man. We're going to watch you for a bit and decide later whether we need anything more than a visit from you."

From the get-go I found myself loving the classroom but unsatisfied with it. Lectures from behind a lectern to young seminarians could not fulfill the divine calling that gripped me. Only sermons from behind a pulpit to "normal" people could accomplish that.

Part of what I cherished about my role as a professor was seeing kingdom potential in my students. I didn't realize it at the time, but in my first semester of teaching, a kindred spirit and eventual partner in both theology and ministry was present. A young man within whom love for truth and love for the lost competed for attention. Commitment to the Bible and keen interest in the cultures unbelievers inhabited cross-pollinated in his mind and heart. There he was, seated right in front of me in that Kansas City classroom, ten years my junior, a young graduate student with scary biceps, in love with biblical truth and aching to plant a church in a city.

His name was Darrin Patrick. Darrin had made his way to Kansas City from southern Illinois, that upside-down pyramid-shaped piece of geography sprinkled with towns bearing names like Thebes and Cairo. Little Egypt, the locals call it, a land settled by migrants from the southern Appalachian mountains of Virginia, Tennessee, and the Carolinas. Culturally speaking, these were my people. On the face of it you wouldn't imagine that either Little Egypt or the foothills of the Blue Ridge Mountains could serve as incubators for urban church planters. But what do we know? Nothing while God still thinks He's God and does whatever He pleases.

Darrin was an excellent student who graduated almost as soon as he completed the one theology course he took from me. His name and face faded into the fog of the more than seventy students who passed through my classrooms each semester. Lots of water would pass under the bridge before our paths would cross again. I would quit America for Asia, believing that if I did come back to the United States, it would be to the promised land (the South), not the Midwest. But God knew everything. All the days meant for King David—and for Darrin and for me and for you—were written in His book before one of them came to be (Ps. 139). Twelve years later, Darrin Patrick would reemerge out of the fog and change not only my life, but the lives of many.

Chapter Two

FEELING OUT THE FADED GLORY

Everything's up-to-date in Kansas City.
They've gone about as fer as they can go.
Rodgers and Hammerstein, *Oklahoma!*

The sanctuary of First Calvary Baptist Church captivated my imagination from the moment I crossed the threshold into its hauntingly beautiful worship space. A dimly lit space, yes, but not dreary, not at all. Its tempered light reflected off of deeply carved woodwork, heavy and ornate, that was set off by upholstery and thick draperies of burgundy and gold.

The eye travels up the vaulted ceiling to a cupola—recessed, windowed, framed, and crossed by carved wood. Stained glass surrounds the worshippers closest to the pulpit, and above pulpit and baptistery shines a round window of beveled glass whose burst of color refracts through the image of an open Bible. Stout organ pipes frame pulpit and baptistery. A balcony looms in back and extends its two arms along both sidewalls to become an exquisite gallery hanging just above the preacher's eye level.

GLORY DAYS

Able to accommodate just over six hundred worshippers, the sanctuary was a mini Spurgeon's Tabernacle plunked down in the Westport section of midtown Kansas City. Westport was the site where, from the 1830s—four years before the Town of Kansas was founded—thousands of starry-eyed pioneers set off westward on the Santa Fe Trail in search of a new life. At Westport in 1864, in the still-new frontier of the spanking-New World, the U.S. Army forces of Major General Samuel R. Curtis defeated Major General Sterling Price's outnumbered Confederate soldiers in the "Gettysburg of Missouri." There, in the midst of all that history, sat this gem of a church house—heavy gray limestone and sandstone, accessed through over-size oak doors, enclosing a worship space crying out for prayers and baptisms, weddings and funerals, and especially the proclamation of the gospel of Jesus Christ. I had the privilege to preach there just one Lord's day in the absence of the interim pastor. Or so I thought.

> Imagine those pews full and those pipes resonant again. What an exhilarating worship experience must have been enjoyed each Lord's day in First Calvary's heyday, when two morning services held a congregation that could exceed a thousand persons.
>
> —Darrin

Amid the wagon trains headed west, a group of eighteen followers of Jesus Christ gathered on July 4, 1840, to constitute the Regular Baptist Church of Big Blue, Jackson County, Missouri. This was the beginning of what, by 1994 (when I arrived in Kansas City), would be known as First Calvary Baptist Church. But by 1994, the thousand worshippers who once filled the sanctuary had dwindled to a remnant.

I was transfixed and smitten. Having grown up on the wrong side of the tracks in the Deep South, in the cocoon of a culture—formerly agricultural but now upwardly mobile blue-collar Southern Baptists—I knew that most of those who had worshipped at First Calvary were not "my people," not "my kind of Baptists." These had once been uptown Baptists, white-collar professionals, small-business owners, civic leaders, patrons of the arts. Some were bona fide movers and shakers in greater Kansas City.

The church of Jesus Christ is not a building; it is people. But First Calvary's magnificent sanctuary was not just a building either. It commanded a historic and still-strategic outpost on the frontier of gospel advances namely within one of the increasingly secular cities of America, which are now among the fastest-growing mission fields on the planet.

I found myself unable to contemplate this declining flock with nonchalance. At stake were not mere bricks and stained glass, but the advance of the light against encroaching spiritual darkness.

FADED GLORY

By the time I accepted an invitation to preach at First Calvary, the glory days of that congregation were past but not forgotten. Not by those who had invested time, tithe, and talent in the ministries that once flourished there. But those days themselves were long gone, and First Calvary had settled into the all-too-typical downward slide toward congregational death.

For some twenty-five years, most measurable indices of ecclesial health had fallen at First Calvary: membership, attendance, baptisms, financial support, missions giving, and mission activity. When churches settle into extended periods of decline, they sometimes adopt a defensive rhetoric that touts spiritual growth or spiritual health over numerical growth. Such false dichotomy often masks a tragic loss of vision, a lapse into spiritual sloth, and even defeat. Numerical growth can never substitute for spiritual health and may even cloak spiritual rot. But true spiritual health always longs to see the body of Christ grow. It longs to see the joy of the gospel shared and to offer more praise to its Lord.

> From 2000 to 2007 only four states saw numeric growth in the percentage of the population attending an established church (i.e., one more than forty years old).
>
> —Darrin

Only a tiny percentage of churches that sink to a certain depth ever truly recover. In the vast majority of cases, prolonged decline proves terminal.[2] Close to 8 percent of all churches in North America have reached a plateau or are declining.[3] The vast majority of most churches' growth comes from people switching churches. Only a small percentage (1 to 3 percent) of the growth comes from conversions.[4]

First Calvary was into its third decade of decline. One had to reach back to the 1970s to find a pastor who enjoyed sufficient congregational support to lead the church in any serious sense. In the decade before I came, First Calvary saw the arrival and departure of eight men: four pastors and four interim pastors. The man who served just before my tenure lasted a mere ten months.

Thom Rainer's book *Breakout Churches* sparked in me an epiphany of pessimism about churches like First Calvary. I smelled the

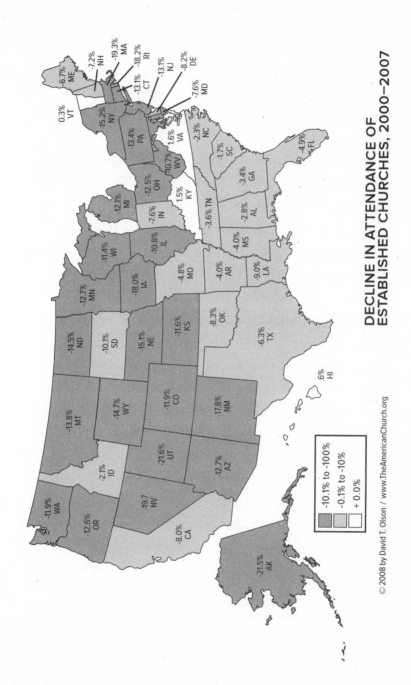

DECLINE IN ATTENDANCE OF
ESTABLISHED CHURCHES, 2000–2007

-10.1% to -100%
-0.1% to -10%
+ 0.0%

© 2008 by David T. Olson / www.TheAmericanChurch.org

whiff of death there. The book suggested that apart from unusual new leadership and a new movement of the Spirit of God, First Calvary was doomed. Rainer highlights congregations that have recovered from long decline but also makes clear how rarely such recoveries occur.

So I carried a bit of a doomsday head of steam into my interim and then into my bivocational pastorate at First Calvary. Though I experienced twinges of guilt, I believe this gloomy outlook served me well. I doubt that the rescue of First Calvary could have been accomplished had I marched forward in cocky triumphalism during the early days of my service there.

IRRESISTIBLE INTRIGUE

Having settled in Kansas City in 1994 to take up a teaching post at Midwestern Baptist Theological Seminary, I visited First Calvary with my family in search of a new church home. Because of distance and other factors, we ended up elsewhere, but First Calvary retained a hold upon my imagination. Long before I was invited to preach there, I seized upon any news of it. Yet I did not set foot there again until September of 2001, just before the horrific events of 9/11. I was fresh from a stint of missionary service in Bangkok, Thailand, and one of my colleagues at Midwestern—then serving as interim pastor at First Calvary—asked me to preach in his absence.

The worship space retained its allure, but during the six years since my last visit, the congregation had lost many members. Within weeks I was invited to take up interim pastoral duties after my friend resigned to accept a teaching post in another state. Although I had served as pastor and interim pastor of several churches over the years, assumption of pastoral duties at First Calvary felt different to me from the beginning. There was my long-standing intrigue associated with the worship space and with its urban setting. Also, two members of the search committee that had recommended me for the vacated post emphasized the need for strong pastoral leadership at this sensitive juncture.

Additionally, I sensed this congregation's strategic importance. It stood in midtown Kansas City, which had a virtual absence of vital evangelical witness in its urban core and the urban areas bordering that core.

> All contexts—suburban, rural, and urban—need new churches. But there is a special need for new churches in cities. By planting and replanting churches in urban centers, we have a strategic opportunity to influence the entire world, because the entire world is coming to live in, work in, and visit cities.
>
> —Darrin

This opportunity weighed on me as I considered my duty to this body of believers and to God. I felt that failure here would be a more tragic loss for the gospel than I had discerned elsewhere. On the other hand, success here promised to bring a great cause for rejoicing.

Yet divine intervention alone could bring health and growth to First Calvary. Revitalization would require major changes. Significant change almost always meets resistance and generates relational pain. Resistance and relational pain almost always sabotage efforts to lead through significant change.[5] If I attempted to lead this church where I thought it ought to go, I knew I would likely find myself walking into the teeth of an ecclesiastical monster capable of chewing me up and spitting me out. That had already happened to more than one former pastor who had dared to challenge the status quo.

I was exhilarated and apprehensive. On the one hand, I was captivated by dreams of what might be possible for this congregation and the surrounding community. Many urban communities were finding new life as yuppies (young urban professionals) and DINKs (dual income, no kids), and a variety of unmarrieds were choosing to take up residence in cities rather than escape to the suburbs. Such developments bring new resources, both financial and human, that sometimes render urban soil less resistant to church planting especially because, for many of these new urbanites, the desire to live within a more ethnically, racially, and culturally diverse setting is a significant part of their attraction to the city. Bordered on one side by a neighborhood in transition and on the other by a revitalizing residential and entertainment district, First Calvary struck me as a strategic resource for kingdom advance and for my denomination.

On the other hand, too often urban settings were vast graveyards for churches, especially for Bible-believing, theologically orthodox congregations. The ghosts of many well-meaning, committed pastors and church planters haunted the urban landscape. I did not relish the prospect of joining their ranks. So why did I hazard such forbidding terrain? Part of the answer is history.

THE PROMISE AND BURDEN OF HISTORY

As a professor of theology and church history, I celebrate our indebtedness to our forebearers in the faith. We didn't discover the gospel of Jesus Christ. They bequeathed it to us. By their sacrifices and obedience—and also through their brokenness, missteps, and failures—they have given us models and warnings that should enrich our faith and guide us in our own callings. They belong to that great cloud of witnesses in Hebrews 11–12 whose faithfulness in trial and suffering ought to strengthen us in our own challenges. And where spiritual blindness, rebellion, abandonment of the gospel, or lapse into idolatry punctuate the history of God's people, God expects these episodes to be retained in our collective memory. Why? Because "these things took place as examples for us" (1 Cor. 10:6; Heb. 3:1–4:13).

That First Calvary Baptist Church was 160 years old when I first settled into the pastor's study only heightened my awe and wonder and sense of duty. For decades, Southern Baptists sang from the *Broadman Hymnal* as they worshipped Sunday mornings, Sunday evenings, and Wednesday nights. *Broadman* conflates the surnames of two of the four founders of the first Southern Baptist theological seminary. It was launched in the mountainous northern reaches of Greenville County, South Carolina, on the eve of the War Between the States in 1859, and John A. *Broad*us and Basil *Man*ly Jr. made up half of the founding theological quartet.

Several times per week since childhood I had reached for these hymnbooks, once ubiquitous in Southern Baptist life. They were

embossed with the hybrid title *Broadman*. In friendly competition
with the Bible, this hymnal had stamped my theological and pastoral
identity. On Sunday, September 21, 1890, John A. Broadus had
preached the dedicatory sermon for the newly constructed worship
center of Calvary Baptist Church. The history of First Calvary was
precious and personal for me, and it was also strategically important
for the spiritual revitalization God was preparing.

PREACHER KILLER

I always do research on any congregation that extends a call to me. But
never had I encountered a church with so much history not only open
to historical inquiry but also in need of it. First Calvary's past weighed
heavily on its present and its future prospects. Several of my colleagues
at Midwestern Baptist Seminary had served as interim pastors there,
acquaintances had been members of that congregation, and many
others I met possessed detailed knowledge of the historic church. I
pumped them all for information. The picture that materialized was
fascinating and frightening. For all its storied accomplishments in a
century and a half, by 1994 First Calvary had earned a reputation as
having become something of a preacher-killing church.

First Calvary was embedded within a secularized urban context
on the edge of a neighborhood in transition. It was a shrinking community of faith composed mainly of members who commuted great
distances to reach the church on Sunday mornings. It was saddled
with a still-magnificent but now deteriorating worship center and an
equally at-risk educational complex more suited to a bygone era than
to the challenges of twenty-first–century urban America. Most

importantly, it was largely controlled by a handful of powerful lay members habituated to having their way and resistant to pastoral leadership.

I sat across from two of these powerful laypersons, Jeff and Keith, early one Saturday morning at a chic local café. Jeff was a retired businessman now serving as the paid part-time administrator of the church. Jeff would tell whoever might listen that God had called him to the ministry earlier in life, and now he was finally obeying that long-suppressed prompting of the Holy Spirit. Administrate he did: in the early days, staff meetings took place in his office with Jeff presiding from behind his desk while the pastor (i.e., me), the minister of music, and the youth minister dutifully scribbled notes on little paper pads. This was before the days of iPhones and iPads.

> One diagnostic test to determine if your church is a candidate for a replant is to look at the number of pastors who have led it in the last thirty years. Churches in need of a restart have often had short pastoral tenures and a series of interims.
>
> —Darrin

And there was Keith as well, fingering his half-consumed cup of manly black coffee over the remains of a wholly consumed omelet; a nearing but not-yet-fully retired businessman in possession (at least in his own self-estimation) of worldly wisdom and savvy along with the concomitant advantages and superiority that wisdom and savvy won for him in relation to any preacher he had ever encountered. "Preachers just don't understand how the world works." But not to worry—Keith was here and at my disposal.

The message Jeff and Keith delivered to me suggested (or did it?) authentic openness to leadership and even change: "Dr. DeVine, we are not ready to put together a search committee for a permanent pastor. This congregation needs time to heal under a long-term interim pastorate. We need more than a preacher right now. We need pastoral care and strong pastoral leadership."

It's not unusual for influential laypersons to express such strong desire for pastoral leadership and to mean it—in a way. But this bold plea for leadership could not be taken at face value. What counts as leadership is in the eye of the beholder. This café conversation marked only an initial step on a winding path toward comprehension and confrontation.

TAKING THE PLUNGE

I accepted the invitation to go to First Calvary as interim pastor. I did so with skepticism about the congregation's prospects. The urban setting, the neighborhood in transition, the money pit of a facility, and the four entrenched and power-jealous laypersons, and only a movement of the Holy Spirit could overcome such obstacles.

So why did I accept the call? History was part of it but so was habit. If I'm not preaching at least forty to forty-five weeks per year, I don't know what to do with myself. After thirty-two years of ministry,

> Despite the church-growth movement and the proliferation of megachurches, over half the congregations in America are composed of fewer than a hundred worshippers on a given Sunday.
>
> —Darrin

I remain astounded at the opportunity to preach the Word of God to the people of God and see them embrace the mission of God. Rejecting opportunities to preach does not belong to my makeup.

But another church had invited me to serve as their interim pastor too. Never had this happened to me before. Because of my fear of First Calvary, I tried to gain a good conscience as I contemplated accepting the other invitation. I could not do so. I was held back.

I felt free to accept First Calvary's invitation, because I do not believe a declining church is necessarily an evil, an embarrassment, or a spiritual dead end. I expected that once I began to preach at First Calvary and became a part of the family of God there, I would discover wonderful, Bible-believing brothers and sisters in Christ. That is just what I found. Breezy, dismissive attitudes toward troubled churches facing decline are misguided. These are our brothers and sisters in Christ. They are precious in the Lord's sight, and ministry among them is worthy.

Approximate Distribution of U.S. Protestant and Other Christian Churches by size[6] (excluding Catholic/Orthodox)

ATTENDANCE	# OF CHURCHES	WEEKLY WORSHIPERS	PERCENT
7–99	177,000	9 million	59%
100–499	105,000	25 million	35%
500–999	12,000	9 million	4%
1,000–1,999	6,000	8 million	2%
2,000–9,999	1,170	4 million	.4%
10,000–plus	40	.7 million	.01%
TOTALS	approx. 300,000	approx. 56 million	100%

Larger churches bring missionary vitality to the body of Christ, but smaller churches continue to provide the bulk of ministry, evangelism, pastoral care, and missionary work on planet Earth. Nothing suggests that this setup will change anytime soon.

Still, I found myself unable to assume a benevolent, hospice-care attitude toward First Calvary. My respect for the congregation was not complemented by much hope for its future. I was in a state of heightened alertness, diagnosing the community's condition, spinning out mental scenarios by which the church might be saved. Unconsciously at first, I strategized for its rescue.

The first piece of that strategy crystallized with chilling clarity. I had to face the ecclesiastical monster with four sets of hands locked in a death grip around the levers of power. No happy future I could imagine could arise until those hands were removed. They were unlikely to loosen their grip willingly. A metaphorical claw hammer might have to be employed.

Chapter Three

DISSECTING DYSFUNCTION

And why were those haughty nobles destroyed and with that
utter destruction? Why were they scattered over the face of the
earth, their titles abolished, their escutcheons defaced, their parks
wasted, their palaces dismantled, their heritage given to strangers?
Because they had not sympathy with the people, no discernment
of the signs of their time; because in the pride and narrowness of
their hearts, they called those whose warnings might have saved
them theorists and speculators; because they refused all concessions
till the time had arrived when no concessions would avail.

Thomas Babington Macaulay

Effective leadership of a church typically involves casting a vision for the congregation. By *vision* I mean a picture of what it might look like for a particular band of believers to live and serve as the people of God here and now. Not a vision conjured out of the musings of the pastor's head but one received from God. And not usually a vision received like a bolt of lightning from beyond, untethered from Bible and tradition. Rather, a vision received from the God of Abraham, Isaac, and Jacob, the Father of our Lord Jesus Christ; a vision received from the only God, Creator of heaven and earth, who has spoken and who yet speaks, who continues to fulfill His revealed plans for His people and this world, who remains faithful to His ancient words and deeds. A vision, therefore, both nurtured by and answerable to God as He speaks through the Bible and the church's history since the resurrection.

Contemporary vision casting is caught up in a real history of God's dealings with His church. Pastors are not called to slap a monotonous spinning wheel as though history repeats itself. Nor does the would-be vision caster fumble around with a dusty old set of supposedly unchanging tried-and-true instructions for effective leadership. Rather, vision casting calls for discernment here and now—discernment undergirded, guided, warned, and tested by the authoritative Word of almighty God in Holy Scripture. It asks this question: Given God's revelation, what is required of us here and now, in this time and place, for the advancement of the gospel and the building up of the body of Christ?

But no casted vision achieves incarnation in this world unless and until it is embraced by the congregation. Pastoral leadership always requires leadership of people—actual flesh-and-bone, namable, locatable persons. So wherever I lead a church, I ask: What are the names of the people, the fewest number of people, who, if I lead them, will enable me to lead the entire congregation? If I lead these two or five or ten folks, I shall take the whole flock with me. But if I cannot lead these, I might call my efforts "leadership," but in reality I'll just be taking a walk by myself. At First Calvary, compiling the list of names took me about five weeks.

THE LAY CARTEL

Four members of First Calvary wielded disproportionate influence over that congregation. We have met two of them already, Keith and

Jeff. Two women also exerted significant power. There was Sandra—sharp, gregarious, classy, confident, organizer extraordinaire, and teacher of the largest and most active Sunday school class in the church, and who was utterly at home in the spotlight, happy (like me and surely most preachers) hearing the sound of her own voice reverberate before a rapt audience. And there was Pam, no less organized than Sandra, with an enormous capacity for work, as responsible as the day is long, bonded with and protective of the magnificent worship space, with labyrinthine roots in the church that extended not only to lay members but to former pastors and staff.

These four—Keith, Jeff, Sandra, and Pam—sometimes as individuals, periodically in collaboration, acted as the gatekeepers and power brokers at First Calvary. Each, over decades, had consciously and unconsciously marked out their turf. Each parcel of this ecclesial territory was guarded with practiced and sometimes surreptitious zeal. The machinations of these four, in spite of their good intentions, did not result in genuine leadership of the church. Rather, they rendered the church unleadable—certainly unleadable by any pastor anyway.

> The main reason churches fail is poor leadership. Pastors and lay leaders can fail to lead the church well through their mishandling of the Scriptures, failing to take biblical truth seriously. Pastors and lay leaders can also fail to lead well through mishandling of people, failing to take conflict and cultural change seriously.
>
> —Darrin

It was not that these four agreed with one another on most issues or were even the best of friends most of the time. But whatever divided them, on one matter their thinking coalesced: they would circle the wagons to prevent any pastor from truly leading the congregation. They behaved like a lay cartel.

Time would prove that Keith and Jeff's strongly articulated quest for robust pastoral leadership came with a gigantic asterisk. What the cartel really sought, or at least what their actions aimed at, was a pastor who would discharge certain discrete duties (among which anything resembling strong leadership was not included), keep his hands off their turf, and be accountable to them for the congregation's health and growth. They wanted a pastor to preach, protect the property rights of the cartel, and accept responsibility *as though* he were lead pastor.

Each of the four deeply loved First Calvary. Each was heavily invested in it, having served the congregation tirelessly for decades. None of the four meant harm. But intentions aside, as a group, they had drifted into pernicious patterns of behavior that had paralyzed the church administratively and spiritually. As a result, successive pastors gave up and moved on. The church continued its downward plunge.

I became convinced that, before God, accepting a call to lead First Calvary meant committing to dethrone the cartel. That meant almost certain failure. Not failure adorned with some heroic afterglow, but failure fraught with second-guessing and finger-pointing. It was easy to envision myself walking away from First Calvary a few months down the road as though from a smoking crater left by a bomb I had detonated, a crater where a living congregation had once worshipped and prayed together.

Why not just walk away immediately? Or why not accept a call to permanent part-time status but forget about these doomed dreams? Why not just provide the kind of noble and riskless hospice care some congregations can stand without implosion? Efforts to confront the cartel might accelerate the church's death. Who did I think I was? The cartel members were fixtures of the church, some for fifty or sixty years. Would any prudent man dare challenge such an entrenched syndicate?

NO TURNING BACK

> Jesus said to him, "No one who puts his hand to the
> plow and looks back is fit for the kingdom of God."
> (Luke 9:62)

I challenged it with my eyes open. Several factors convinced me.

First, unless the current power structure was dismantled, the gospel witness would eventually die at the corner of 39th Street and Baltimore Avenue. It wasn't dead yet; a flickering wick of missional vision still burned. A precious circle of elderly women constantly reached out to the nearby neighborhoods where they lived. They gave themselves utterly to every new and prospective member. A couple within the congregation opened their home to international exchange students from the nearby university and brought a stream of international believers and unbelievers into the church. But the supply of spiritual oxygen to these small but valiant clusters of spiritual energy was slowly being cut off.

The prevailing culture of the place, despite a superficial sheen of interest in the gospel, expended its energies largely in nostalgia, defense of personal perks and privileges, and the sabotage of would-be pastoral leadership. The more I researched the recent past of the church and examined its present state, the more convinced I became that only radical steps—including multiple and likely bitter confrontations with the lay cartel—held out much hope for spiritual revival.

Was this conviction presumptuous? Did it betray doubt in the power of the God who can create children of Abraham from stones? Perhaps, but my heart was disturbed by the decline of churches across North America, many strikingly similar to First Calvary. Maybe God was showing His providence precisely by seizing my mind with concern for First Calvary. I tried, but I could not escape the conviction that God had planted in me this persistent—and in my experience unprecedented—preoccupation with the future of this local body of believers. And the cartel was the unavoidable roadblock to that future.

My second reason for confronting the cartel was that it was my job. I had sat across from the members of the interim search committee as they expressed the church's need for strong pastoral leadership. I had embraced that duty. No one had forced this burden upon me. I had knowingly welcomed the task of leadership at First Calvary before God and many witnesses. There was nowhere to hide. The buck stopped with me. I knew it, and I knew God knew I knew it.

Third, I had a strategy by which a new future for the church might become possible. Nothing like this had ever seized my imagination at other churches where I had served—at least not with such relentless clarity. I lost sleep due to sheer exhilaration. I believed I was involved in the work of the Lord. The thrill waxed and waned, but it persisted during the eventful days that lay ahead.

My final reason was that the unique circumstances of my call to First Calvary meant I could take on the cartel without risking my family. I'm not proud of this contributing factor, but it's important to get this out on the table. I doubt I would have been willing and able to take on the task that faced me at First Calvary had my family been on the scene with me. I'll never know that for certain. But one of the most daunting duties of a pastor's is providing leadership in a setting where their family members are present and vulnerable. Where else do we make such a demand of our leaders?

> At some point, leaders in a declining or plateauing church have to look at themselves in the mirror and say, "Enough is enough." Leaders need clarity about what the Scripture says the church ought to be and courage to stand against those who refuse to let the Scripture inform their view of the church.
>
> —Darrin

My admiration for pastors has always been high, and one reason is this special burden of having to negotiate the terrain of leadership—and spiritual leadership, no less—when those most precious to him are so exposed to the fallout of his and others' decisions. I faced no such circumstance at First Calvary—not directly at least.

I was a member of a small population of preachers whose calling regularly takes them away from their immediate families and into a growing mission field—the interim pastorate. Even though my formal status at First Calvary morphed from a simple interim into a bivocational pastorate, my role was always to prepare the church for a pastor who would lead it in ways my other day job couldn't permit.

As the percentage of churches struggling with decline continues to rise, the frequency of interim periods between permanent pastors increases and the duration of these interim periods is lengthening. Such conditions expose an alarming spiritual decline. But they also offer possibilities for repentance and revitalization. This new mission field is fraught with deep spiritual pathology and entrenched dysfunction. But below the surface of the aimlessness lies real resources for spiritual rebirth. We worship a God who loves to move mightily in just such circumstances, not least because they provide perfect backdrops for the display of His glory and our utter dependence on His grace.

CONGREGATIONAL CHAOS

As time passed, it dawned on members of the cartel that I was serious about my leadership responsibilities in ways Keith and Jeff had not anticipated. I began to discuss the prevailing structures of decision making in various settings: with the deacons, with individual members or pairs of the cartel. I asked probing questions meant to highlight the connection between healthy pastoral leadership and effective evangelism and discipleship among sister churches. I seized opportunities to raise questions related to church discipline and noted that church discipline was sanctioned in the governing documents of the church. I asked whether any of the present leaders could recall actual concern about or practice of such discipline during their decades at the church. I used various settings—committees, the board, and even the pulpit—to explore how certain features of the open weekly business meeting could undermine the recruitment of gifted laypersons to serve in vital ministry positions (see Appendix B). The cartel's collective radar detected an alien in its midst.

Might control over their fiefdoms face a threat? Covert maneuvering commenced.

One day I asked the cartel what happened to the church's last long-term pastor. He had won admiration from the congregation as a whole. His preaching was widely appreciated. He'd had a vision for how the congregation might again have a gospel impact in Westport. Despite the quality of his character and preaching and despite the loyalty so many in the church felt toward him and his leadership, he chose to leave. Why? The answer, in part, was that the cartel had repeatedly frustrated his efforts to exercise leadership.

> One of the harsh realities of declining churches is that well-intentioned people unrighteously begin to see themselves as the controllers of the church instead of servants to the church. These controllers hasten the church's death.
>
> —Darrin

My question to the cartel was deliberately open-ended: "What happened? Why did this man leave?"

After offering a smidgen of praise for this former pastor, the cartel coalesced around their view of the events that had led to his departure: "He started trying to run the church."

When a mangled version of congregational rule grows up and settles in, the admonition of Hebrews 13:17 goes unheeded—"Obey your leaders and submit to them, for they are keeping watch over your souls, as those who will have to give an account." To the cartel, staff did not exist to generate ideas, cast vision, strategize, determine the direction of the congregation, or reshape the ministries of First Calvary. Staff were employees hired to perform ministry tasks the cartel thought necessary.

I asked about this former pastor several times, and key people always eventually found their way back to the crux of the complaint: "He started trying to run the church." This charge ought, in their minds, prove sufficient for any true Baptist, protective as they are of democratic, congregational church governance. The congregation, not any one man, has responsibility for—and therefore must have control of—the local church. Too often such self-satisfied smoke screens, while feigning protectiveness of tradition and denomination, obscure a jealous grip—not by the congregation as a whole, not by a long shot, but rather by a very few pairs of determined hands around the levers of congregational power.

I inquired further. This popular former pastor was not known as a hard-driving, autocratic, controlling person at all. In fact, he and I became personally acquainted, and a stereotypical power-hungry control freak he was not. Yet in the mind of the cartel, "trying to run the church" accounted well enough for the sad but finally prudent and inevitable departure of this otherwise well-loved minister.

Unless declining, congregationally governed churches rethink knee-jerk resistance to strong pastoral leadership, they can usually kiss hopes of revival and growth good-bye. Prudent but genuine delegation of duties to a pastor need not constitute a shirking of congregational responsibility but rather the proper and biblical discharging of that sacred duty.

I probed more deeply into the cartel's pat answer: "He started trying to run the church."

"Do you mean," I asked, "that this former pastor wanted to have his way on the most important, most strategic matters affecting the future of the church he was called to lead and be held responsible for?"

The answer was yes.

I used various settings to explore the nature of leadership with select church members within the congregation. I wanted them to see that First Calvary had drifted unwittingly into a pattern of power sharing that formally called for pastoral leadership but had, in fact, ceded veto power to the cartel.

One tool the cartel wielded was control of that most-hallowed arena of congregational rule: the monthly open business meeting.

Chapter Four

THE DEVIL'S WORKSHOP

"I will show him how much he must
suffer for the sake of my name."

The Lord to Ananias about Saul (Acts 9:16)

"You meant evil against me, but God meant it for good."

Joseph to his brothers (Gen. 50:20)

THE INVISIBLE HAND OF THE ALMIGHTY

When I arrived at First Calvary, the monthly open business meeting often produced congregational chaos. But praise be to our God who loves to hit straight with crooked sticks. The swirling cauldron of upset and inefficiency that was the business meeting played a pivotal role in the rescue of the gospel at 39th and Baltimore.

Gradually but persistently, I tried to lead the congregation. The cartel's radar detected encroachments on its territory. After three years, Keith decided I had to be reined in or pushed out. He dipped into a tried-and-true bag of tricks to thwart me: the constitution and bylaws of First Calvary Baptist Church combined with a heavy dose of *Robert's Rules of Order*. Keith thought he had discovered a procedural oversight during the recent hiring of a new youth minister,

Joshua. John, a respected attorney in the congregation, kept detailed notes related to this matter.

Joshua had already passed through various stages of the vetting process. He had been interviewed by the personnel committee that Keith himself chaired and on which I sat as pastor in an ex officio capacity. We voted unanimously within the committee to recommend Joshua's hiring at the next business meeting. Virtually every regular attender of the business meeting knew that the personnel committee would recommend hiring Joshua, who was already an active and well-received member of the church. Yet, between the conclusion of the committee meeting and the looming business meeting, Keith had either produced or stumbled upon a little stick of dynamite he hoped would erode the congregation's trust in me as their pastor. Keith became convinced that the current personnel committee was not authorized to recommend Joshua's hiring in the business meeting.

> The emotional cost of a replant is enormous. The leaders must be ready to take friendly fire masquerading as concern for the church.
>
> —Darrin

Keith planned to make the procedural misstep in Joshua's hiring (had he set a deliberate trap?) known at the upcoming business meeting and insist that Joshua not be hired or receive pay until the error could be corrected. In Keith's mind, the correction needed would take another month or more to complete. The unacknowledged purpose of all this was to embarrass me in front of the congregation.

Cartel member Jeff, the septuagenarian church administrator, had come to feel affection for me personally and to appreciate certain facets of my ministry. He knew of Keith's plan and struggled with whether to alert me to the impending confrontation. Would Jeff remain loyal to the cartel, or would he, as a paid member of the ministry team at First Calvary, warn me? At the last possible moment, Jeff contacted me by phone, alerted me to Keith's plans, and warned me not to oppose Keith's motion at the business meeting.

I pointed out that Keith was implicated in the debacle he had discovered. Because of Keith's committee responsibilities, he should have made me aware of the oversight months earlier when he first became aware of it. I told Jeff that should Keith proceed with his disruptive plans, I would ask Keith why he had not informed me much earlier and in private so as to avoid the unnecessary upset at a public business meeting.

Meanwhile, I consulted with John. He insisted that there was nothing in our governing documents to prevent us from correcting our mistake on the spot, and nothing that required Joshua's hiring, compensation, and continued ministry be compromised in any way.

> In order for a replant to succeed, the leaders must be familiar with what the Bible teaches about the church and almost as familiar with the bylaws of the particular church.
>
> —Darrin

So the stage was set. The cartel, personified by Keith, supported from the shadows by Jeff, and now threatened by my presence, would attempt to stake its claim.

SHOWDOWN

The business meeting ensued on Wednesday evening. Keith rose to address the church and state his case. John kept meticulous notes:

> Keith stood and asked when the personnel committee had met to consider the matter. Mark replied that it was in December, and Keith said that members of the personnel committee were elected for the new year and that the "constitution and bylaws" required these newly elected committee members to make any personnel decisions and therefore the recommendation was not valid. I then asked to speak and pointed out that the personnel committee was a standing committee, only a third of the members were newly elected, and that nothing in the church's organizational documents prevented the committee's actions from carrying over into the new year.
>
> Keith immediately backed off and said he forgot the personnel committee was a standing committee, so I made a motion to hire the new youth minister with or without the personnel committee's recommendation. The motion was seconded and (I believe) unanimously approved.
>
> Mark then asked Keith why, if he had a problem with the recommendation, had he not discussed it with him (Mark) prior to the meeting, choosing

instead to confront him in the meeting and try to undermine his authority. Keith vehemently denied that he had any plans to disrupt the meeting and just wanted to make sure everything was done correctly.

I asked Keith how long he had known about this procedural infraction. He confirmed that he had known for months. I asked why he had not alerted me to the situation immediately, as committee responsibilities and common courtesy required. Keith said it was not his place to tell me. His responsibility was to the church. "But you did share this information with Jeff, did you not? Why to Jeff and not me?" I asked.

The moment this exchange occurred, the prospects for First Calvary's future improved dramatically. Keith's scheming disingenuousness was exposed and would not be forgotten by those present, even by many who had known and been friends with him for decades.

When I did not back down, Jeff stood up to defend Keith and confront me for exposing his warning me of Keith's plans. Exasperated, I countered. Jeff defaulted to a tactic he had used before. He said, "I offer my resignation!"

"I accept," I said.

For a few moments it was as though all the oxygen had left the room. Two or three scattered hands rose to mouths agape. When he experienced opposition or criticism, Jeff often reflexively employed passive-aggressive threats to resign. Such episodes inevitably ended with detractors backing off and yielding to Jeff's wishes. This time, I hadn't played ball.

Jeff and Keith marched machine-like out of the meeting room into the labyrinthine facility where they were heard shouting at one another. The business meeting proceeded. John assured us that the matter could be disposed of at once without violating our governing documents. It was done. The meeting adjourned. Stunned and mainly silent members roused themselves from shock and drifted out into the waning light of dusk.

We knew life would never be the same at First Calvary. We could not know what the future would bring, only that a page had turned and a new chapter had opened that none of us anticipated.

After most members were gone, I made my way toward the parking lot. There was Jeff, lying in wait, hesitant. Stunned that I had called his bluff, he hoped that I might reconsider and rescind my acceptance of his resignation. I told him I would reconsider and give him a definitive answer the next morning.

Prayerfully, dreamlike, I drove the nine miles to my home. I crossed the Missouri River just at the bend where its southward plunge from the far reaches of Montana cuts sharply west on a 250-mile bifurcation of the Show-Me State. A hopeful tranquility hovered over the scene. I felt utterly alive. It was one of the few and precious times during the long journey at First Calvary when I was allowed to believe that the same God who called forth the land by speaking, who made the ostrich just to watch him run, who orchestrates every twist of the Big Muddy, might do something new and spectacular at 39th and Baltimore.

I called Jeff early in the morning to reassert my acceptance of his resignation. Jeff's rethinking of his hasty offer signaled neither a willingness to accept my authority as pastor nor a commitment to support the kind of changes I was convinced were needed. I sincerely thanked him for his many years of service. Jeff cooperated fully during his transition out of First Calvary, doing what he could to hand things off to his replacement in an efficient and cordial manner. For this, I and the congregation owe Jeff much gratitude.

Chapter Five

ASSISTED SUICIDE

[There is] a time to tear down.

The Preacher of Ecclesiastes (3:3 NIV)

No one takes [my life] from me, but I lay it down of my own accord.

Jesus of Nazareth (John 10:18)

THE BEAUTY OF ESTABLISHED POLICY

Local church constitutions, bylaws, and written policies too often become the hobgoblins of mean little minds. This need not be so. In most cases, minimalist governing documents are the best kind. First Calvary's governing documents were minimalist, addressing as little as possible and elaborating as little as possible on what they did address. Yet right there in black-and-white, enshrined with as much "legal" force as such documents can muster, was this little explosive sentence: "The Deacons, in conjunction with the Pastor of the church, shall constitute a Committee on Discipline."

Certain deacons at First Calvary took umbrage at Keith's behavior during the business meeting. These men initiated disciplinary action and removed Keith from active participation on the deacon board. Stipulations for his continued membership at First Calvary were delivered to him in writing:

Dear Keith:

On Monday, February 9, the deacons of First Calvary Baptist Church met for their regular monthly meeting. During the meeting, the deacons convened as a Committee on Discipline under the authority granted by Article 3, Section 2 of First Calvary's Bylaws.

The deacons heard testimony and concluded that you have deliberately challenged and have sought to undermine the authority of our pastor, Dr. Mark DeVine. Such conduct is inconsistent with the position of deacon under the guidelines set out in 1 Timothy. Therefore, the deacons voted unanimously to terminate your service as an active deacon.

We invite you to continue to worship with our First Calvary family if you are willing to submit to the authority of our pastor and stir no dissension among the members. If you have any questions or would like to discuss the decision of the deacons, the officers will be glad to meet with you at a mutually convenient time.

In affirmation of our pastor and to confirm the unanimity of our decision, this letter has been signed by each deacon who was present at the meeting.

The letter was signed by all fourteen active deacons.

I am still stunned by the deacons' actions. Before the watershed business meeting, I acted under the assumption that my efforts would likely fail. I saw little hope that the real power brokers in the congregation could be brought to embrace my vision for First Calvary. Instead, I saw mounting opposition to my efforts to lead. But now prominent members of the congregation were rallying around me. They made difficult decisions under a sense of moral obligation without my prompting. They showed faith and hope that God might do something new and surprising among us. I learned later that key noncartel members met periodically following the pivotal business meeting to discuss whether and how they might respond to the cartel's maneuverings aimed at my demise.

The history of church discipline is littered with the wreckage of lives and faith communities that were torn apart to no good end. Church discipline is only as advisable as the competence, faithfulness, and character of those charged with implementing it. It is only as effective and redemptive as God's activity and blessing afford.

When biblical foundations are weak and the administrators of discipline are insufficiently trained or wrongly motivated, church discipline typically proves disastrous. But church discipline is rooted in Holy Scripture and nurtures the healthy growth of the body of Christ. Badly administered, it leaves mangled lives and congregations in its wake, but so does the neglect of discipline. Where individuals and groups in a church run roughshod over others, the gospel loses its power in the church and its credibility with unbelievers.

> One of the leaders of the Protestant Reformation, John Calvin, said church discipline, unapologetic preaching of the Word, and faithful administration of the sacraments were all marks of a biblical local church. In a declining church, church discipline is nonexistent. But the clear biblical identification of church discipline as a necessary dimension of healthy congregational life should stand as a warning for communities of faith that neglect its judicious administration.
>
> —C

Keith lay low for a while, but eventually he hatched another plot to undermine my leadership and that of the deacon board, which included many people who had been his friends for thirty or forty years. Keith waited for a Sunday when the minister of education and I were both absent, then launched a verbal attack upon us in the largest and most influential Sunday school class, violating his deacon-board–imposed probation. The deacons dealt with him as redemptively as possible, pleading with him to confess and repent. Once again Keith refused. The consequences are recorded in the board's minutes:

> The deacons of First Calvary Baptist Church met on August 15, August 22, and August 29, 2004, as a Committee on Discipline under the authority granted by Article 3, Section 2 of First Calvary's bylaws. The deacons voted by a vote of 14 to 2 to expel [Keith] from membership and remove his name from the roll. Therefore, effective August 29, 2004, [Keith] is no longer a member of First Calvary Baptist Church.

With great integrity, the deacons applied restorative discipline as taught in the Bible. Because of their integrity, most church members, while disturbed and saddened by Keith's expulsion, understood that this serious step was necessary.

To state what happened in this straightforward manner is technically accurate, but the matter-of-factness fails to capture how miraculous it was. That such a consensus could emerge in such a congregation about disciplining such a revered member marks a wondrous occurrence. I still think, *How but by the hand of God could any of this have happened?*

Three years ago while on business in Kansas City, I attended one of the now-packed worship services at the site of the old First Calvary. An enfeebled and saintly member saw me, made her way toward me as quickly as her infirmities allowed, took my face in her hands, and said, "Can you believe what we witnessed here? Can you believe what has happened here?"

COAST-TO-COAST ENCOURAGEMENT

After one exhausting day, I sat heavily in my special chair at home, musing on the fantastically small odds of success my vision faced. I felt utterly alone. The phone rang. A man whose name I had never heard, a former member of First Calvary, was calling from Washington State. He had heard what had transpired at First Calvary in recent weeks and wanted to confirm these things as well as offer his congratulations and support for my leadership there.

Less than an hour later, another former member called from Washington, DC. His message was virtually identical. There I was, in the geographical center of North America, flirting with self-pity, and two strangers from the two Washingtons of the two coasts called to encourage me. God had my attention. The prospect of a spiritually healthy future for this congregation seemed less impossible.

THE CARTEL'S LAST GASP

The cartel had been cut in half. Pam and Sandra remained. Sandra's husband, a deacon, accounted for one of the two no votes on Keith's expulsion. A few weeks after Keith's ouster, Sandra and Pam began phoning me and visiting my office to complain about my having "taken over the church." Some version of this complaint—"he's try-ing to run the church"—rests in the collective Baptist holster for periodic use when a pastor called to lead encroaches on protected lay-ecclesiastical turf.

I pointed out to the two that it was the deacons, who had been Sandra's and Keith's friends for many years, who had initiated and carried out Keith's disciplining. Baptist polity prevailing at First Calvary—shot through with heavy doses of democracy, constitu-tional adherence, and genuflection before the bylaws—had all been meticulously adhered to. I had not pursued Keith's removal. So Sandra's and Pam's quest to attribute the "trouble" in the church to me and my influence was thwarted.

Exasperated, Sandra hurled a question at me that must have been in the minds of many in the church: "How have you swept in here and gained such a following? We have been serving this church since before you were born!"

Ironically, part of the answer lies in the sympathy Keith's mali-cious intrigue had secured for me. Key members recognized that what Keith had done was inexcusable and could not be ignored if First Calvary were to remain a church in anything but name only.

Thanks to Sandra, the pattern set by Keith would continue. She demanded to address the next monthly business meeting to express her outrage at what was happening. On several occasions, select deacons and I urged Sandra to give up her plan, but she refused. We decided to let her speak. The church's tradition and her standing in the congregation led us to conclude that to deny her the opportunity to speak could cast aspersion on the deacons and me. We had conducted ourselves well in Keith's disciplining and did not relish the spectacle of being seen as muzzling a longtime member and servant of First Calvary. In addition, because we had handled Keith fairly, Sandra's determination to impugn that process could backfire.

And backfire it did. The business meeting came. Sandra ranted and embarrassed herself behind the microphone. A few weeks later, furious and humiliated, she left the church in disgust, never to return.

A pattern had emerged, a valuable lesson for church leadership: give the right person the right amount of rope at just the right time, and they might, in undoing their own misguided aims, achieve good things for the people of God.

Chapter Six

I'M NOT THE MAN

This is the land of which I swore to Abraham, to Issac, and
to Jacob, "I will give it to your offspring." I have let you
see it with your eyes, but you shall not go over there.
The Lord to Moses (Deut. 34:4)

In the wake of Sandra's departure, I realized I may have become the single most influential individual at First Calvary. The cartel lay in shambles. Pam alone remained. Now what? The ministry of tearing down bears little resemblance to that of building up.

My responsibility before God to this church weighed on my heart. I had argued that First Calvary needed a pastor with the trust, influence, and structural tools to lead. Now First Calvary had such a pastor, and it was me.

But I had never envisioned myself as the best person to develop a strategy for growth. I had accepted the call as pastor because I had believed the cartel was the chief obstacle to a bright future and because I was willing to attempt dismantling it. Now that the cartel's defeat was essentially complete, what about that future? The next step was to secure the right man to lead the church forward. But how could that right fit between congregation and pastor be found?

The usual procedure for finding a new pastor, would, in my estimation, have little chance for success. Under normal circumstances, the sitting pastor would resign and leave the scene. The congregation left behind would elect a pastor search committee, which would then obtain candidate résumés, listen to trial sermons on CD or view video recordings, and possibly attend a trial sermon by a prospective pastor at a "neutral site," then interview candidates viewed as promising, and at length, present a candidate to the entire congregation for consideration. The candidate would then preach one or more trial sermons to the congregation, be interviewed by the membership at large, and then be voted on. There could be variations in that scenario, but the steps for calling a pastor would follow this basic pattern.

So why not walk away and let such a scenario play itself out? Three convictions prevented me from doing so.

First, I believed the calling of a pastor would be the determinative factor, from a human standpoint, that would shape the church's immediate future. Choose the wrong man, call a leader who was incompatible with this church at this place and time, and prospects for renewal could rapidly evaporate. Few members at First Calvary would have disagreed with this conviction at that time. First Calvary simply had to make every effort to stop the revolving door of short-tenured, frustrated pastors that had preceded my arrival.

Second, I was persuaded that none of us at First Calvary, including myself, possessed the knowledge, wisdom, and preparation to identify fit candidates for this unique intersection of congregation and context. For a Baptist, this was a controversial conviction. Yet I could not shake it. First Calvary, like so many churches, had been in decline for decades. It had lost its ability to keep a pastor. The pastor who preceded me had lasted less than a year. The cartel's machinations had habituated the church to entrenched administrative dysfunction. Add to these problems the dismal track record of evangelical churches in urban settings, and the difficulty of securing just the right pastor seemed obvious.

Third, even if First Calvary called the right pastor, his prospects for success would be jeopardized by the same deficits that made the wise choice so unlikely—lack of congregational wisdom and preparedness. Too often, where congregational rule joins hands with the open monthly business meeting, church leadership boils down to who controls that meeting. And at First Calvary, a handful of laypersons, reflecting disparate and even opposing agendas, had developed over many years an uncanny ability to thwart pastoral attempts to lead. The congregation had lacked genuine leadership for decades. Staff were treated as mere employees with duties assigned by the cartel. A discernible path to a pastor's freedom to lead didn't exist at First Calvary.

> Urban soil is the most difficult place for any church to grow. Yet the majority of churches that need replanting are in the urban core. This is a tough paradox to work with.
>
> —Darrin

Hypothetically, a pastor might, over time, gain the congregation's trust and help them become a leadable band of believers. But a quarter century of failed attempts invited me to consider alternative paths. Given the looming threat of crushing deferred maintenance needs, time was of the essence. Incremental solutions seemed naive, but a more radical overturning of the status quo held real prospects for hope.

The breakup of the cartel had opened a crack in First Calvary's phalanx of pernicious power, but the cartel's demise left a congregation seemingly stuck in cycles of dysfunction with only faded memories of how to be a healthy church. As my diagnosis darkened, so my prescription for recovery grew more radical. Dead churches litter the urban landscape of North America. New church plants (not formerly declining but now revitalized congregations) are the few bright spots in urban America and elsewhere for good reason. In many cases the very conditions that led to a church's decline also render incremental remedies futile. Often only radical cures provide real hope for recovery. If blind, bound, spiritually dead sinners require release from bondage and new birth, should it surprise us that dysfunctional churches often demand dramatic measures to bring about needed change? They, too, need to be born again.

Chapter Seven

MERGER MANIA

Two are better than one, because they have a good reward for their toil. For if they fall, one will lift up his fellow. But woe to him who is alone when he falls and has not another to lift him up! … And though a man might prevail against one who is alone, two will withstand him—a threefold cord is not quickly broken.

The Preacher of Ecclesiastes (4:9–12)

New birth comes from above, not from here below. We can petition God for it, but we cannot execute it. By the grace of God, First Calvary transitioned from a dismal preoccupation with the cartel to the more positive matter of calling a pastor. A bit of sunshine pierced the darkness of the ongoing business of dismantling.

But if we, the members of First Calvary, were not equipped to select the next pastor, who was? Who could find suitable candidates? Should we commence the usual predatory survey of sitting pastors? A dislodgeable pastor could indicate a dissatisfied pastor anxious to bolt and determined to fit the stated qualifications.

What if, instead, we looked at proven, satisfied pastors with no interest in moving? What if we looked for known, accomplished leaders of strong congregations within our own community? What if First Calvary, as a congregation, were to *join* one of these congregations? What if we merged with a strong congregation led by an established, effective, known, and trusted pastor within greater Kansas City? What if First Calvary launched not a mere pastor search but a congregation search?

THE MULTISITE MOVEMENT

My concerns over First Calvary's future sent me into more than two years of research, discussion, and prayer. Early on I learned of the multisite movement. Some congregations, mostly but not exclusively large ones, rather than planting independent self-supporting churches, planted new branches of the mother church. Could this model serve kingdom purposes in Westport? Such new site plants took on a variety of configurations according to the visions of the sponsoring congregations. Some branch sites conduct their own on-site worship services except for the sermon, which is piped in via satellite or delivered via DVD from the mother church.

> One of the innovations of the twenty-first–century church is the use of video technology to distribute sermons. While some have thought video preaching was a fad, it is becoming a mainstay in many growing churches.
>
> —Darrin

Other multisite churches dispatch a preaching pastor for each new site. Still others, where it's geographically feasible, have the mother church's preaching pastor travel to each site personally and deliver the weekly message live.

What if one of the larger churches in our area would consider taking First Calvary on as a satellite congregation? Could First

Calvary be merged with this larger congregation? Many factors attracted me to such a possibility. First, several churches in the greater Kansas City area were potential candidates to do a friendly takeover of First Calvary. Several of these churches were theologically compatible with First Calvary. Their pastors and congregations were well known to First Calvary's members. This familiarity could help build trust among our people. Name recognition of these prominent congregations could boost First Calvary's profile after a merger. Also, these congregations might be able to send a contingent of members from their churches, infusing First Calvary with fresh spiritual vitality and facilitating the launch of a replanted faith community. If initial efforts to restart the church foundered, these stronger congregations would be better prepared to suffer a setback and try again than a traditional church plant might be, especially one blessed and saddled with a strategically situated, magnificent, but deteriorating facility. Resilience could prove an essential ingredient to our successful replant.

LEST THE SEED DIE

Such a merger would also immediately shift decision-making power to the larger parent church. I believed that divesting First Calvary of its ongoing self-determination would be one of the most troublesome but crucial steps to our recovery. I say ongoing self-determination, because the current congregation would have to voluntarily, in standard democratic Baptist fashion, choose to relinquish control over its own future—or at least let go of the tools of self-determination to which it was accustomed. Would this band of believers, in one grand final use of its collective prerogative of self-determination, surrender that power once and for all? Would this Baptist church, metaphorically speaking, fall on its sword as a church? Why would a congregation do such a thing? Why should they?

To survive. In order to keep the proclamation of the gospel, the discipling of believers, and the worship of the only true God alive at First Calvary, First Calvary might have to die. Martyred Lutheran pastor Dietrich Bonhoeffer once said, "When Christ calls a man, he bids him come and die." Could, on occasion, the same be said of a congregation? I think so. One occasionally hears of such a radical relinquishment, but not usually by a congregation still drawing just under a hundred souls on a Lord's day. Although the church's spiritual prognosis was dire, the congregation left in the wreckage of the cartel's collapse remained larger than the average American church.

But must a congregation literally descend into the last stages of its life, drawing its very last spiritual gasps, before considering the risk of a transplant operation? Why shouldn't a radical remedy attractive to a church of eight be applicable to a church of eighty?

Life through death is one the most beautiful paradoxes revealed in the life and teaching of Jesus Christ. He died that we might live, and because He yet lives, so do we. This is how the world actually works. I believed that this paradox held the clue to the way forward for First Calvary.

Yet any move on my part to nudge the congregation in such a direction would evoke surprise, concern, skepticism, and challenge: Why such draconian steps? Why not look for a strong congregation willing to revitalize First Calvary as a mission project, leaving First Calvary in full possession of its autonomy?

Perhaps such a strategy could have worked. I have heard of successful revitalization efforts. But my conviction was that the particular conditions at First Calvary, shaped by her history and recent traumas, rendered merger and replant a much more promising option than some more conventional course.

In many cases, requests for a revitalizing mission effort sound better to the needy congregation involved than to the stronger one. For the stronger congregation, such a request might sound like this: "Hey, we've been failing with our resources for several decades. Why not hand over some of your resources so we can fail with them for a while?" In fact, a relatively robust congregation in North Kansas City was then engaged in a more conventional revitalizing effort with a weaker congregation in Northland. But I was convinced that our urban setting and crumbling physical plant would make it hard, if not impossible, to find a strong, willing, and theologically suitable partner for that. I did not believe that First Calvary's current state stemmed from lack of resources. It stemmed from a deep loss of vision and direction, abdication of responsibility, habitual dysfunction, and loss of living memory of healthy functioning.

I was convinced that what First Calvary actually needed matched what a potential mother congregation would want to hear. The merger and replant I had in mind would result, once the ink dried, in the utter collapse of First Calvary into the hands of the mother church. The mother church would own all assets of First Calvary and have the right to fire all current staff, including myself. With a wife and two sons at home to support, the prospect of losing more than a third of my income sent chills up my spine and gave me pause.

I got in God's face over these personal matters. His answers were already familiar to me: "Be not anxious." "Your Father knows that you need these things." "You are worth more than many sparrows." I was unable to embrace these answers as often or as tightly as I should have. But I did not turn back.

ECCLESIASTICAL SELF-DENIAL

The risks to First Calvary were profound. Once the merger became final, the members would lose the power of congregational self-determination. Should members oppose decisions made by their new mother church, no monthly business meeting would provide the kind of platform to effect change to which they were accustomed. If appeals to the new decision-makers failed, they could withdraw financial support or leave or both. No other recourse of protest would remain. The name of the church would likely be changed to match that of the mother church or to some other name the new leaders deemed appropriate. Following a merger, the mother church could eventually decide that investment in a new ministry at 39th and Baltimore might not be the best stewardship of their limited resources after all. In a worst-case scenario, the facility could be sold

> In every kingdom endeavor, there is a time and a place for raw faith. A time to risk comfort, security, and all you have known for the reward of seeing God do something unexplainable.
>
> —Darrin

and the ministry abandoned. Still, in my mind, the existential threat already looming over First Calvary justified the risks. If two congregations decide to walk into the future together as partners and God joins them, the result could reflect the insight of the Preacher—"a threefold cord is not quickly broken" (Eccles. 4:12).

I searched for a theologically compatible Southern Baptist church in Kansas City that might entertain the possibility of a merger with First Calvary. I searched alone and secretly at first. Should none of the pastors of candidate churches express willingness to explore the possibility, the last thing I needed was a congregation made hopeful only to be freshly disappointed. Nor would premature opposition to a hypothetical merger serve any good purpose.

Four local pastors showed real interest. These four congregations either already had or were planning to launch additional worship sites. My plan would offer them certain unusual features for a church plant. It would provide an aesthetically striking worship space of a sort especially favored by a growing contingent of believers in their twenties and thirties. True, our facilities had costly maintenance issues, both ongoing and deferred, but the worship space and site held historic significance for Baptists in Kansas City, and it was located in the Westport section of midtown where signs of urban renewal held unique opportunities for new ministry. Young professionals were moving into this popular entertainment district situated just a few blocks north of the famed Country Club Plaza.

The opportunity to be part of a successful church plant in the heart of Kansas City intrigued these already-effective church leaders. These men could not easily forego this chance of making such a contribution to their beloved city. Three of them looked long and hard at the opportunity. They were drawn to it. They wanted to want to do it. Surely a merger and replant of First Calvary could work for their congregations.

Yet one by one, the initial enthusiasm of each waned. At length, each said no. Various factors played into these decisions. But in each case, the real deal breaker was the same the cultural factor. Each of these men had proven track records of effective ministry. Their personalities and leadership styles differed, but each had demonstrated great leadership abilities. Yet their success occurred in suburban contexts. They realized that effective ministry in the suburbs predicts little or nothing about prospects for the city. They knew that where effective evangelism and church planting are concerned, culture matters.

International cross-cultural ministry demands special capabilities and training. Increasingly, church planters here at home have to face the cross-cultural realities that shape North America. Rural and suburban believers may sincerely pray for urban neighborhoods crammed with heavily tattooed and body-pierced populations, but few have a clue as to how to evangelize or plant churches among them. Few show the inclination to make the attempt. I started with four potential candidates to merge with and replant First Calvary. Three down. Only one to go.

Chapter Eight

THE SEED DIES

Unless a grain of wheat falls into the earth and dies, it
remains alone; but if it dies, it bears much fruit.
Jesus of Nazareth (John 12:24)

And they all pretend they're orphans
And their memory's like a train
You can see it getting smaller as it pulls away
Tom Waits, "Time"

EASTSIDE AND WESTPORT

Though not located in the urban core of Kansas City, Eastside Baptist occupied transitional terrain in a border area between the petering out of true city and the rise of suburbia. Pastor Kevin Jones, Eastside's pastor, was well known and admired at First Calvary. The two congregations boasted a long-shared and storied history. For a brief stint during the nineteenth century, the same man simultaneously held the pastorate at both churches.

Pastor Jones knew First Calvary and its history well and recognized that a replant in Westport would have to look quite different from the ministry he led at Eastside. The cultural setting of First Calvary would call for a different kind of ministry, not doctrinally but culturally. My talks with Pastor Jones started slowly but soon picked up speed and gained substance. Within a few months it became clear that if I could persuade First Calvary to take the plunge, a merger with Eastside would likely occur.

Pastor Jones brought others in his leadership team into the discussions and, for the first time, I broached the issue with a few leaders at First Calvary. Eventually I assembled a Vision Team representing a cross section of the congregation to pray and think through the possibility of a merger. Within weeks both Pastor Jones and I made our congregations aware of our dream for a merger in which Eastside would assume leadership responsibilities for First Calvary. The name of First Calvary would likely be changed. The ministry at First Calvary would be recast. Several alternative visions for the reshaping of ministry were on the table. Which option would be attempted first would not be determined until probably a few months after the merger was signed, sealed, and delivered. Indeed, all of the discussed options could be scrapped and replaced with something utterly unanticipated.

LEARNING TO SEE

Again the questions forced their way to the surface. How could First Calvary be led to do such a thing? And why should they be so led? Why should a congregation pursue such a radical and irreversible solution to its decline? The justification remained the same. First Calvary should consider a merger in order to resuscitate the advance of the gospel at 39th and Baltimore.

I was convinced, but how could *the congregation* be convinced? My own conviction had become a kind of seeing. I saw that this was the right goal to pursue. When people see something, the time for convincing is past; only acting on the reality remains. Should the congregation come to see what I saw, their action would become automatic.

God had not called me to bully a proud little flock down a path of my choosing. They needed to see what I saw. They needed a new perspective that could embrace a new vision they had never even contemplated. How could such a new perspective be achieved? How could it even be pursued?

We needed not just a new perspective but true perspective. We needed to see the truth about who we were as a people in the sight of God to gain insight into what God required of us and what might please God to do with us. But what does perspective mean? Surely not simply persuading folks to do what I thought was right rather than what they thought was right. No. Perspective indicates a seeing—an unobstructed seeing with a wide scope.

> The book of Proverbs says, "Without vision the people are aimless." The only way for a replant to happen is if people see a preferred future in which the local church is attacking the gates of hell with the glorious light of the gospel.
>
> —Darrin

Lack of perspective arises from failure or refusal to look where one ought to look. The blind spot some vehicles produce can usually be overcome by a combination of mirror positioning and forward leaning—but unless one knows of the blind spot and takes the necessary steps to gain the needed perspective, hidden danger threatens. The opposite of perspective is myopia—the narrowed seeing of only that which is right in front of us.

The spiritual myopia plaguing First Calvary was not that they were stuck in the past, not really. It was that they were stuck with a present and a likely future that remained unillumined by the past. They were paralyzed in a present distorted by a false comprehension of the past. The perspective they lacked was historical perspective. They saw before them a storied sanctuary in need of care but not the story they themselves belonged to. There was no way any of us could gain the perspective we needed apart from retrieving and reentering into the story in which we were already caught up.

This was by God's design. One of the most frequent complaints of God to His people throughout the Scriptures is that they fail to remember. The perspective God expects of us and provides to us brings wideness of vision not only in space but in time, not only future time but also past time. If we at First Calvary were to move forward as God intended, we would have to look back first.

LOOKING BACK TO MOVE FORWARD

The actuarial tables for U.S. churches put the average lifespan of a congregation at around ninety-six years. Nine-and-a-half decades of life; that's about it for most congregations. First Calvary Baptist Church was already in her fifteenth decade when I arrived on the scene in 1998. She had already defied the actuarial tables by more than half a century, and she was living on borrowed time. The two-and-a-half decades of decline that preceded my arrival provided evidence to that effect.

But what about First Calvary's successful defiance of the actuarial tables for more than fifty years? How had she achieved this unusual longevity? Ninety-six years is just an average. Perhaps First Calvary was an exception. Having already far outstripped the typical congregation in longevity, who was to say she could not do so for another half century without major changes?

Startling facts came to light as I researched the church's history. First Calvary's more than 160 years traced back to the founding of the Regular Baptist Church of Big Blue (River) in 1840, which changed its name to United Baptist Church of Big Blue in 1842. After two years this congregation moved to the bustling area that would soon be called Westport. Sometime between 1844 and 1860 the church changed its name to Westport Baptist Church. Meanwhile, across the state line, the First Baptist Church of the Town of Kansas, also known as the "May Street Church" was founded in 1855.

Tensions within the congregation over the Civil War led to the departure of many members, who went on to found Central Baptist Church. By 1872, when animosities generated by the war had largely abated, Central and First Church reunited and met as one at the May Street Church. In 1876, partly because of a dispute over the Lord's Supper and partly because of a long-standing interest by some members to plant a mission church in another part of the city, eighty members withdrew from First Church to found Calvary Baptist Church, which met first at 14th & Locust Street. They built and moved into a new structure at 11th & Grand in 1877 and then into a stunning sanctuary at 9th & Harrison in 1890. It was here that Dr. John A. Broadus, founder of the Southern Baptist Theological Seminary, respected scholar, famed preacher, and teacher of preachers, delivered the dedicatory sermon on the Lord's day, September 21. The history of First Calvary confirms what Timothy George has called "the fissiparous strategy for church growth" in Baptist life: they multiply by dividing.

In 1920 the stream of division was interrupted. The two parent streams claimed by First Calvary Baptist Church came together. Westport Baptist Church was without a pastor and was attracted to the current pastor of Calvary Baptist Church. Calvary wanted to move south, and Westport Baptist's 39th & Baltimore location was judged ideal for their needs. So in October 1921 the two congregations became one, retaining the name Calvary Baptist Church. To distinguish itself from other "Calvary" Baptist churches in the area, the name First Calvary Baptist was adopted in 1983.

The flow chart below depicts this history. That history was complex but also productive. Thousands came to saving faith in Jesus Christ through the ministry of this family of faith. At least fourteen men were licensed to preach. Seventeen were ordained to the gospel ministry. Missionaries with ties to First Calvary, twenty-seven in all, took the gospel to every inhabited continent on earth. KOZY-FM carried the worship services of First Calvary across the airwaves. For many years First Calvary's "Festival of Light" was offered as a gift to the city. Eventually this extravaganza of music and drama had to be staged in Kansas City's Music Hall to accommodate the crowds. Under the auspices of the Southern Baptist Convention and the leadership of Pastor Conrad Willard, Midwestern Baptist Theological Seminary was founded in 1956 with First Calvary providing its facilities to house the new school until new buildings could be erected on a permanent site north of the Missouri River.

FLOW CHART HISTORIES

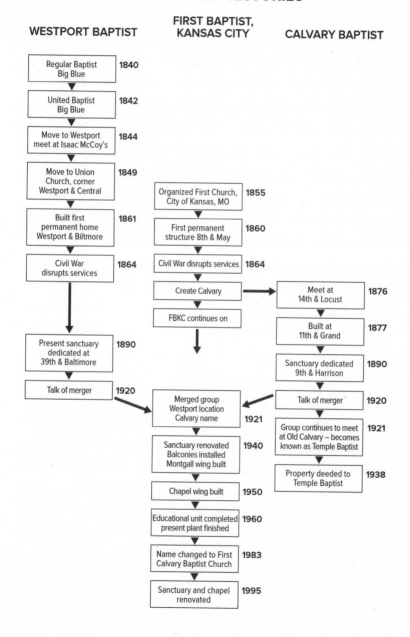

WESTPORT BAPTIST

FIRST BAPTIST, KANSAS CITY

CALVARY BAPTIST

Regular Baptist Big Blue	1840
United Baptist Big Blue	1842
Move to Westport meet at Isaac McCoy's	1844
Move to Union Church, corner Westport & Central	1849
Built first permanent home Westport & Biltmore	1861
Civil War disrupts services	1864
Present sanctuary dedicated at 39th & Baltimore	1890
Talk of merger	1920

First Baptist, Kansas City column:

- Organized First Church, City of Kansas, MO — 1855
- First permanent structure 8th & May — 1860
- Civil War disrupts services — 1864
- Create Calvary
- FBKC continues on
- Merged group Westport location Calvary name — 1921
- Sanctuary renovated Balconies installed Montgall wing built — 1940
- Chapel wing built — 1950
- Educational unit completed present plant finished — 1960
- Name changed to First Calvary Baptist Church — 1983
- Sanctuary and chapel renovated — 1995

Calvary Baptist column:

- Meet at 14th & Locust — 1876
- Built at 11th & Grand — 1877
- Sanctuary dedicated 9th & Harrison — 1890
- Talk of merger — 1920
- Group continues to meet at Old Calvary – becomes known as Temple Baptist — 1921
- Property deeded to Temple Baptist — 1938

MY NEW BEST FRIEND

The means by which the people who became First Calvary Baptist Church had maintained their ministry was a model for our current members and me. First Calvary's defiance of the actuarial tables for local churches had involved all sorts of radical steps. Her history was punctuated with moves, name changes, and mergers. It even included the voluntary death of churches in order to give birth to new congregations. Can anyone find the Regular Baptist Church of Big Blue or United Baptist Church of Big Blue? What about Westport Baptist or the May Street Church? Did they not, sometimes consciously, sometimes less so, sacrifice the immediate shape of their ecclesiastical lives so that the ministry of the Word of God lived on? Had not these people of faith put God's purposes, captured in the Great Commission of our Lord, ahead of treasured congregational configurations and ahead of the particular names that once marked their places on the ecclesial map?

I reflected on that remarkable story of faith. Westport Baptist Church, May Street Church, First Baptist Church of the Town of Kansas, Calvary Baptist Church, First Calvary Baptist Church—all these names figure in that celebrated history that stretched back to eleven years before the Civil War. Mergers and name changes galore.

These mergers and name changes helped explain how First Calvary had exceeded, by a half century, the average longevity of the typical congregation in America. The flow chart drew tears to my eyes, because I was staring at a depiction of divine activity, a witness to the ways of almighty God not just then but now. While many members of First Calvary treasured the congregation's history, none had considered the implications of that history for our present struggles.

Armed with knowledge of First Calvary's history, I was in a position to present this newest twist on merger and name change as old hat for First Calvary. Its older members prized the congregation's history. I largely approved of their pride and protectiveness while recognizing the retrograde uses to which pride and protectiveness could be put. I had expected the suggestion of merger or name change to provoke that pride and a reflexive defensiveness. But to my great surprise, the church's history had just become my new best friend.

Informed loyalty to the tradition at First Calvary defended not its name nor resisted merger but rather abhorred the waning of gospel witness. Faithfulness to tradition at First Calvary would pursue the advance of the gospel and the healthy upbuilding of the church above all else. The worship of almighty God, the making of disciples, the ordination of ministers of the word, the dispatch of missionaries, and service to the

> Evangelical Christians have a tendency to either radically overvalue church history—allowing treasured tradition to trump Scripture instead of letting Scripture have its way with tradition—or radically undervalue church history—believing that what God has done in the past has little to no value in the present. Churches likewise are tempted to misuse their history and fall into "we've never done it that way here before" syndrome. Or they neglect to value the past and fall into the "those who don't learn from history are doomed to repeat it" effect.
>
> —Darrin

community—these were the precious historic treasures meriting protection. The name and location of the church were means to these ends. If First Calvary must, in a sense, die that the gospel might live, so be it. That was tradition at First Calvary! That tradition reflected God's own means of redeeming lost sinners through the death of Jesus Christ on the cross.

Hypothetically, a church's willingness to move, merge, or accept a name change may stem from spiritual weakness, even cowardice. It may expose loss of faith. But it need not do so. Willingness to embark upon such a radical course may reflect courage and willingness to sacrifice born of faith in God's promises. It could reveal the loving sacrifice of what one holds dear for the sake of what one values most. It could be a wise investment of one's resources in the advance of the gospel.

Faith, not cowardice, takes the step into unknown territory for the sake of Jesus Christ and His church. Love, not self-preserving protectiveness, sacrifices its own life that others might live. Hope of new life, not resignation to inevitable decline, yields itself up in the quest for a better future.

On the other hand, when congregations hunker down, fiercely protective of their name or of their power of self-determination as they decline year after year, the act of hunkering down may evidence not courage, steadfastness, or faith, but rather stubbornness, congregational selfishness, and unbelief. They may even reveal idolatrous attachment to that for which Christ did not die, namely a particular local church of a particular name in a particular place. Christ's promise that the gates of Hades shall not prevail against His church remains in effect. When any particular local church dies, Christ's church does not. If a church, in its dying, finds opportunity to invest its resources in such a way that advances the gospel and edifies the church, should it not do so? Faithful stewardship behaves thus. Faith, hope, and love are displayed in such a case.

CONCRETE HOPES

I threw myself full throttle into the pursuit of a merger with Eastside Baptist. Seldom had I felt so utterly alive as a minister of the Word of God. I believed I was doing the work of God for the advance of the gospel. Little by little, key members of First Calvary began to share my confidence and excitement. Prayer and preaching were the mainstays of my efforts. In a sermon I pointed to a large plaque in the shadows of a darkened alcove. The plaque recorded the names of church members who had fallen in the trenches of World War I, members of Westport Baptist Church. Our forebearers in the faith. Would we prove faithful stewards of the inheritance bequeathed to us by these members of the cloud of witnesses?

Over a period of months the two congregations moved closer to a merger. The Vision Team and I presented our case first to the deacon board, which voted unanimously to pursue the merger. Armed now with their support, we brought the matter before the whole church, conducting numerous listening sessions and Q&A forums. I argued that given the dismal prospect for First Calvary apart from a merger, our first question should not be whether the replant of First Calvary would likely suit our own tastes. Indeed, the replanted church would likely not suit some, perhaps even many, of First Calvary's current members. What we were about was the recovery of a robust gospel ministry and the preservation of a viable congregation at 39th and Baltimore, not the preservation of a church to our liking.

By this time, several respected members of the congregation had fully embraced the quest for a merger and were advocating its achievement publicly. The paid staff knew of the plans and understood that their own employment would be jeopardized by the merger just as mine would be. One of these staff members, in response to an objection to the merger, stood up in a business meeting and spoke movingly of the seed that cannot bear fruit unless it dies.

HOPES DASHED

At length, First Calvary voted unanimously to merge with Eastside Baptist Church. Many people nervously awaited the upcoming vote at Eastside that would seal the deal. Some who had voted yes nevertheless had qualms regarding this path.

I was ecstatic. I had believed for more than three years that something like the path we were taking offered the best hope for the rescue of the gospel at First Calvary. Prayer, study, research, conversation, and other events had only strengthened my confidence that we were on the course chosen by hand of the Lord.

I believed that the words of Psalm 139, "in your book were written, every one of them, the days that were formed for me," applied to every person involved in the merger. But I believed even more that I had been allowed to see a bit of what God was doing. God governs this universe with meticulous providence, though He gives us the capacity for decision making. But the details of God's providence usually remain hidden from us. Typically, we only catch glimpses of these details, and even then, usually in retrospect. We walk by faith, not by sight.

Yet from time to time He lets us see His cards. I believed God was allowing me to peer into a tiny crack in the door of divine doings. But I was dead wrong!

A crisis totally unrelated to the impending merger erupted at Eastside. The merger moved from inevitable—merely a matter of time, mere days away—to impossible! The dream was dashed to pieces before our very eyes. Members of First Calvary, while grateful that the trouble at Eastside erupted in time to prevent the merger, now found themselves in worse shape than before talk of a merger surfaced. We lived in the wake of this shocking disappointment as though in a dark crater of our own making. No, of my making, wasn't it? The Devil whispered in my ear, "Who do you think you are? What hubris it took to lead this little flock down this dead-end street! Are you happy now? Just look at the mess you have made!"

SWINGING FOR THE FENCES

By the grace of God, in the days that followed the crushing of our hopes, we were able to rally. I rebuked the Devil—that liar and murderer. I found surprising resources from beyond myself that sustained my spirit and reignited my resolve to work once again for a healthy congregation at First Calvary. Close Christian brothers and sisters committed to pray often for us and for me. Key members were not ready to give up. We continued to pray and dream together. We continued to believe that our God loves to bring new life and might well bring it to us.

The Lord heard our cry, lifted us out of the miry clay, and set our feet, once again, upon a rock (Ps. 40). The collapse of the Eastside merger was a real setback. But the ominous diagnosis of First Calvary's condition remained, and now many members—not just the pastor and the Vision Team—shared it. In addition, First Calvary's unanimous vote to merge with Eastside demonstrated spiritual insight, faith, and courage on the part of a people who, just a few months earlier, had (some knowingly, some not) acquiesced in the debilitating and obstructive maneuverings of the lay cartel. We were in a very different place as a congregation than we had been prior to the months of consideration, labor, and prayer leading up to the vote to merge. A sweet trust and hope now characterized our fellowship in the Lord. I hunkered down once more to serious prayer and thought.

> In every church plant and church replant there are setbacks and closed doors. It is as if the Lord allows us to pursue options that, in our mind, seem perfect, only to take those options away in order to work the humility that will be required for leadership in the long haul.
>
> —Darrin

Three of the four congregations I had identified as potential partners had, in my estimation, wanted to want to move forward with a merger. Yet their pastors drew back. The chief obstacle was the cultural hurdle that would face any suburban congregation attempting to replant a church in an urban setting. I still believe that a merger with Eastside had great potential for success. Pastor Jones was a proven leader committed to evangelism and discipleship who preached the Bible and understood the need to replant First Calvary as a congregation indigenous to the cultural context of Westport.

But now that the Eastside merger was off the table, why not ask a new question? Why not swing for the fences? Why not construct in our imagination the perfect candidate for a merger with First Calvary and then search for such a congregation? Rather than limit consideration to those options familiar to us and near to hand, why not widen the scope of our search to a congregation more precisely suited to Westport itself?

ACTS 29

I searched now not only for evangelicals, preferably Southern Baptists, but also for a pastor who had succeeded in an urban environment similar to Westport. Trust between First Calvary and such a congregation would have to be developed initially without the luxury of proximity and long familiarity, but through deep theological compatibility and demonstrated missional effectiveness.

Mindy, a former student and now a staff member at Midwestern Seminary, uttered nine crucial words: "Why don't you take a look at Acts 29?" Well, partly because the book of Acts contains only twenty-eight chapters! But Acts 29 was a church-planting network founded at Mars Hill Church in Seattle by lead pastor Mark Driscoll.

Mars Hill was not a Southern Baptist Church. In fact, it was not denominationally affiliated at all. But it was Baptistic in the sense that it practiced believer's baptism, not paedobaptism. Theologically, Mars Hill embraced a confessional statement compatible with my own theological convictions. Driscoll himself fervently preached doctrines considered by many to be anathema to younger generations—sin, repentance, and hell. He taught that Jesus Christ is the only hope for the salvation of the world. Biblical teaching on election and predestination were neither sidestepped nor watered down. Driscoll even insisted that the office of pastor or elder should be restricted to male candidates alone. Whatever accounted for the growth of Mars Hill, cowardly genuflection to the winds of cultural political correctness was not it.

Such preaching had not prevented Mars Hill, planted in downtown Seattle, one of the most pagan cites in America, from growing at an astounding rate. It drew exactly the folks his preaching was supposed to repel. Thousands of twenty- and thirtysomethings poured into the Mars Hill worship center, where they heard the Bible taught and the gospel proclaimed. They were called to repent from sin, trust in Jesus Christ as Savior and Lord, and engage in ministry.

Not only was Mars Hill theologically orthodox, evangelical, and reformed, it also took culture seriously, not as a source of revelation but as the context where effective churches must be planted and flourish indigenously. Many theologically conservative congregations assume an us-versus-them attitude toward the culture at large. They retreat into a religious ghetto, viewing the culture outside the walls of the church mainly as a contagion to be avoided. Such a mind-set seems to take with great seriousness the "Be ye separate" dimension of the biblical mandate but finds it difficult to embrace that other mandate with equal fervor: "Go ye into all the world!" or to say with the apostle Paul, "I become all things to all men in order that I might save some."

Driscoll, on the other hand, argued that where the church confronts culture, three possibilities arise. In certain respects, the culture will prove inimical to the gospel, in which case resistance and prophetic calls for repentance are the church's duty. Other dimensions of the culture may be neutral to the gospel or may even prove advantageous to gospel advance. In Thailand, for example, the study of English is wildly popular. Missionaries oblige by teaching English as a second language using the Bible!

Driscoll's comprehension of this case-by-case discernment of the relationship between culture and Christianity struck me as a much better model for negotiating the increasingly complicated urban cultural terrain of North America than either an embattled retreat from culture or a naive, oblivious plunge into culture in which the truth of God is adjusted for and accommodated to the culture. Too often in such cases, political correctness, not faithfulness to Holy Scripture, becomes the predictor and shaper of message and ministry. Driscoll's model seemed to reflect more accurately the actual relationship between culture and gospel. And this model seemed much more capable of faithfulness to both biblical mandates: "Be ye separate," and "Go ye." Anchored theologically in the sixteenth-century Reformation, Mark Driscoll and a growing cadre of young pastors also embrace a passionate commitment to the missionary mandate right here in the United States. They are, to borrow from the title of one of Driscoll's bestselling books, "Reformissionaries."

As I surfed the Acts 29 website, a familiar name caught my eye: Darrin Patrick. Patrick was vice president of Acts 29 and pastor of The Journey, a Southern Baptist congregation in St. Louis, Missouri. St. Louis is about 1,580 miles closer to Kansas City than Seattle!

Patrick founded The Journey in 2002 with thirty people. By 2006 the church had grown to seven hundred in attendance in two locations. As this volume goes to press, The Journey has grown to six locations and has released seven church plants. Best of all, the original location looked very much like midtown Kansas City and Westport. I clicked the link for Darrin's personal information, and the mystery of his familiarity was solved. Darrin graduated from Midwestern Baptist Theological Seminary during my first year of teaching there.

I dug out my old files from those days and there he was, my former student, summa cum laude graduate, first in his class, who loved theology and the Bible and churned with a passion for urban church planting even then. The more I learned about The Journey,

> One of the surprising things I discovered in helping lead Acts 29 was the openness of denominational leaders and established churches to share their facilities with new church plants. I believe God is connecting the generations through humble leaders who want the gospel to progress through the local church for emerging generations.
>
> —Darrin

the more excited I became. Finally, in March of 2006, I made the phone call to Darrin Patrick. Soon the story of First Calvary became a story embracing not just the one but the two great cities of the Show-Me State.

Chapter Nine

DECISIONS AND DREAMS

And he said to me, "Son of man, can these bones live?" And I answered, "O Lord GOD, you know." Then he said to me, "Prophesy over these bones, and say to them, O dry bones, hear the word of the LORD. Thus says the Lord GOD to these bones: Behold, I will cause breath to enter you, and you shall live. And I will lay sinews upon you, and will cause flesh to come upon you, and cover you with skin, and put breath in you, and you shall live, and you shall know that I am the LORD."

So I prophesied as I was commanded. And as I prophesied, there was a sound, and behold, a rattling, and the bones came together, bone to its bone. And I looked, and behold, there were sinews on them, and flesh had come upon them, and skin had covered them. But there was no breath in them. Then he said to me, "Prophesy to the breath; prophesy, son of man, and say to the breath, Thus says the Lord GOD: Come from the four winds, O breath, and breathe on these slain, that they may live." So I prophesied as he commanded me, and the breath came into them, and they lived and stood on their feet, an exceedingly great army.

Ezekiel the Prophet (Ezek. 37:3–10)

My conversations with Darrin went well. We had a natural affinity. Those intangibles of personality that can make or break a relationship over time worked for us rather than against us. A major basis for this compatibility was that theology did not compete for attention in our minds and hearts with practical issues such as evangelism, discipleship, church planting, and church growth. For both of us, biblical, theological, and practical matters inextricably belong together.

Also, both of us believed we were living the dream. Little in our backgrounds suggested the futures that now beckoned us. Each of us had landed in wild unimaginable adventures not of our own making, and we both relished them.

From the very beginning, Darrin responded positively to my zany musings about a cross-state merger. This is Darrin's default posture toward most any exciting challenge—take it on. Success rarely gives birth to timidity. Turn Darrin loose, other elders at The Journey had learned, and they might find themselves buried under paralyzing commitments far and wide.

Discernment by a plurality of elders rather than a lone pastor offers many benefits. Periodic and prudent fires can be lit under the overly cautious. The reflexively but sometimes recklessly bold can be reined in. At least one member of the elder board in St. Louis judiciously restrained Darrin's willingness to take on the world.

Nevertheless, we inched forward in our discussions. I would attempt to lead members of First Calvary to merge with (and be engulfed by) The Journey. Practical control of First Calvary would shift to The Journey. The Journey would own all of our assets. All current staff at First Calvary would serve at the pleasure of The Journey. We dreamed together of a partnership in ministry that spanned the state of Missouri. With fear and trembling, longing and exhilaration, we eased into a future none of us could have imagined possible.

THE PITCH

The Journey elders invited me to St. Louis to worship, meet, talk, and pray. I mingled anonymously before the worship service at their Hanley Road venue. I made my way up to a crowded balcony, settled into a packed pew, breathed in deeply, and waited to see for myself if what I had read and heard was true.

I drifted into a trancelike state. Distance from home typically opens up my spirit as if I'm on retreat. I yielded to the worship of God with strangers, many of whom were a decade or two my junior.

I fought back tears. The room rang with the singing voices of God's children. The sanctuary was filled with twenty- and thirty-year-old urbanites, ostensibly unreachable postmoderns,

The timing of these lofty discussions about helping Mark nurse this sick church back to health was unbelievably bad. My entrepreneurial capacity for new opportunities had served The Journey well. Not only had The Journey been able to plant an autonomous church of its own, we had also started training dozens of pastors each quarter from multiple denominations and networks. Acts 29 was growing as well, demanding much travel from me as I was tasked with decentralizing our network into regions all over the country. The Journey itself had grown to seven hundred people in two locations, and we were getting ready to add a third in West County, St. Louis. We certainly didn't need, as more than one of our elders remarked, "to plant another church in West-west St. Louis, also known as Kansas City."

—Darrin

especially through the kind of no-holds-barred Bible teaching Darrin was offering. There they were, row upon row, hunched forward, Bibles open, brows furrowed, drinking in every word spoken by my new favorite preacher from Little Egypt. Yearning gripped me. This, exactly this, is what I wanted to see 250 miles west at 39th and Baltimore. It was a God thing.

We couldn't snatch up what I longingly witnessed in St. Louis and plunk it down in Kansas City, but I could—with a new clarity—petition almighty God for exactly what I wanted and what only He could bring about.

CRACKS IN THE CONSENSUS

Back in Kansas City, only the Vision Team knew of the overtures I had made toward the elders at The Journey. We decided that unanimity among ourselves must be prerequisite to moving forward. Better for the rest of the members never to hear of The Journey than to broach the merger idea prematurely and risk precipitating a nasty split in the congregation. Better to achieve consensus among our team and gain confidence that The Journey had embraced the idea before drawing others at First Calvary into the mix. After the Eastside debacle, another raising and dashing of hopes was the last thing we needed.

After what I had experienced in St. Louis, my weekly mounting of the pulpit at First Calvary took on new energy and urgency. Fresh from daily wrestlings with God, I envisioned a packed house of youngish Bible-toting urbanites drinking in the Word of God and committed to a life of following Jesus Christ. I had visions of an invasion of life-giving witness in Westport, and this vision seemed less and less a mirage. It seemed to be coming at us—not something that needed construction so much as something demanding adjustment, obedience, and gratitude.

Doubts surfaced in the Vision Team. The Eastside fiasco weighed on the minds of some. Had that partnership been legally sealed before scandal befell Eastside, where would it have left us? Had we not learned our lesson? Why shouldn't the appalling collapse of the Eastside merger be recognized as God's merciful rescue and warning? Was not God calling His little flock back to well-worn paths of struggle and decline and away from wild and almost-certainly delusional dreams?

What could these young preacher boys from St. Louis know about ministering to elderly brothers and sisters in Christ? What about the 250 miles separating the two churches? Did not geography alone pose an insuperable obstacle to true fellowship between First Calvary and The Journey? While these forebodings did not derail the Vision Team, they agitated frequently enough to cast a pall over our meetings.

One man, Charles, wanted to leave the Vision Team without giving a clear reason. For six years he had been a stalwart supporter of my leadership at First Calvary. The saga of the cartel had won his loyalty to me and given him courage to stand beside me. I persuaded Charles not to leave the Vision Team just yet. But his face, once the picture of trust, now projected emotional distance and even suspicion. I was at a loss. What could possibly account for this transformation? Charles confided in another Vision Team member, who in turn confided in me. "He thinks you made up The Journey."

During the initial stages of my contacts with the St. Louis church, I instructed Vision Team members not to visit The Journey. Just as our Vision Team at First Calvary wished to control the timing of broaching a possible merger with our members, so did elders at The Journey among their members. My presence in St. Louis was easily accounted for. I was brought in to lead the elders in the study of a book I had recently published on Dietrich Bonhoeffer. In time, of course, all Vision Team members and all members at First Calvary would be encouraged to visit worship services at The Journey.

Nevertheless, Charles found my instructions against visits suspicious. He had to be in St. Louis on other business and decided to defy the commitment the Vision Team had made. He determined to track down The Journey, worship there, and see for himself what I might soon nudge First Calvary to hook up with. But to no avail. Charles could not find The Journey! A local minister acquaintance told Charles that he remembered such a church in St. Louis, but that it had closed. Charles was shocked and then incensed. His own pastor had concocted an imaginary congregation as partner for a merger! To what end was anyone's guess.

Perhaps Charles felt he could not confront me directly. That would expose his own surreptitious defiance of our agreement to put off visits to The Journey for a time.

I raised the issue with Charles at a Vision Team meeting and, amazingly, he stuck by his guns. "I think you made it up, Pastor," Charles said. "Until I see it with my own eyes, I will not believe it."

I believed him. His face was set.

After this, I happily gave my blessing to Charles's permanent departure from the Vision Team. Oddly perhaps, this episode with Charles marked one of the most positive turning points of my time at First Calvary. Charles's betrayal increased my confidence that God Himself would merge The Journey with First Calvary. My assurance increased dramatically when I encountered the Devil's opposition right in front of my face. Of course, I had been sure that God would facilitate the Eastside merger too! Clearly, I was insufficiently humbled by that previous failure of discernment. Nevertheless, my confidence soared, though this time perhaps shot through with traces of a more sober awareness that ultimately God's ways remain to us inscrutable. Though much work, much obedience of faith, many happy duties fall to us, in the end it behooves us to watch and, in the words of W. A. Criswell, "see what God does."

CHUMMY AND CHEEKY

My newfound peace about the matter displayed itself in a meeting with The Journey elders in St. Louis. We shared lunch at a local restaurant and assessed where we were in our discussions. The continued growth of The Journey, together with ongoing projects and immediate challenges they faced, made the timing of a merger problematic. I agreed to present a scenario to the Vision Team according to their timing even though my preference was to move forward decisively. The Journey was not yet ready to move forward—what else could we do but wait? Few biblical injunctions occur with more frequency than this one: wait upon the Lord!

More fundamental concerns also surfaced in our meeting. Like Darrin, other key leaders of The Journey were married men in their thirties with growing families. They were already burning the candle at both ends, struggling to cast vision for the future, meet the growing demands of a growing ministry, and be faithful fathers and husbands. Why take on some optional, distant, risk-laden opportunity? Why now? Why ever? My response was that everyone at the table recognized that The Journey was better equipped to respond to the challenges First Calvary faced than any other candidate we knew of. I even expressed my sympathy for the elders who would soon decide the matter.

> One of our elders, a sales guy by trade, was really concerned about this potential partnership. His argument was that The Journey was doing a terrible job of pastoring and discipling its own people and that adding a new church across the state would not improve this reality. This highlights the counterintuitive fact that it is just as difficult for a growing church to partner with a declining church as vice versa.
>
> —Darrin

The elders' concerns and hesitancies were far from trivial. The Journey had not consciously put itself into a position to replant a church 250 miles away. Our congregations found themselves at an intersection of our formerly separate histories neither had anticipated but in which both sides now recognized the hand of God.

Chapter Ten

GIVING UP CONTROL

Obey your leaders and submit to them, for they are keeping watch
over your souls, as those who will have to give an account.
The Author of Hebrews (13:17)

The elders in St. Louis took the plunge. They would proceed to explore a merger, and if things went well, they would do it. They would do it according to their timetable, but God willing, they would do it.

A series of listening sessions and Q&A forums with Darrin and First Calvary were scheduled. These proved vital to First Calvary's learning process as a merger was now contemplated in earnest. Blunt talk about the radical consequences of such a merger forced the congregation once again to revisit the deepest questions about what it means to be followers of Jesus Christ, to be a local body of believers, and to be stewards of resources that ultimately belong not to us but to God. Jesus said, "For whoever would save his life will lose it, but whoever loses his life for my sake and the gospel's will save it" (Mark 8:35). This applies to local churches as well as individuals.

The governing documents of The Journey and the confirming testimony of Darrin himself made clear that, theologically, we were compatible congregations. But going forward, The Journey could not guarantee the preservation of any particular cherished, long-standing programs or projects. Under Darrin's leadership, a newly designed ministry strategy would be launched. There would be no business meetings where First Calvary members could either micromanage or reject that strategy. Opposition to the new strategy could be expressed in two ways: withholding financial support or departure from the fellowship altogether.

The harsh reality was that First Calvary had to surrender control and trust the Lord through the growing church. Both churches would take a huge risk but would do so because reaching their community for Christ was worth it.

Our folks at First Calvary did not flinch. Apparently the vote to merge with Eastside had lanced the boil of jealousy over congregational decision-making prerogatives that some churches would rather die than relinquish. Darrin's unmistakably genuine passion for the gospel, his track record of effectiveness, his poise and affability, his obvious leadership ability, his years of habituation to the Baptist psyche, and a myriad of intangibles that matter so much where weighty and highly emotional commitments are at stake—all these coalesced to win from First Calvary the one indispensable ingredient: trust.

We realized that we trusted Darrin Patrick enough to take the leap, if only we might hold his hands on the way down. The new desire at First Calvary was to convince Darrin himself to move to Kansas City and lead us. But God had other plans. On September 30, 2007, The Journey became the owner (in human, and thus limited, terms) of First Calvary Baptist Church. It was a friendly takeover. We eased into a new adventure with eyes wide open. The search for a church planter commenced in earnest.

I had nothing to do with the search and next to nothing to do with the selection of the next pastor of First Calvary. Though years now separated my initial intention to coax First Calvary into a merger of some sort, my desire to shift responsibility for the eventual pastoral search and selection had not waned. My head hit my pillow with a long-forgotten sweetness the night following the day we sealed the shifting of that responsibility.

Others, not I or the current members of First Calvary, had to choose the pastor or replanter of the new congregation. Darrin was, after all, the highfalutin vice president of the ballyhooed Acts 29 network of church planters, the shaper of church-planting boot camps across the country to which wide-eyed church-planting wannabes voluntarily submitted themselves for coldly objective assessments in the form of rigid and unfeeling letter grades. "Let Darrin the Discerner strut his stuff," I said. "And let me sleep."

Happy is the person or family or church that accurately discerns when and when not to doctor itself. Why throw good money away when a string tied to an aching tooth on one end and a swinging door-knob on the other suffices for a cure? But woe to the person or family or church that refuses to cry "HELP!" in the face of serious injury or disease. Too many Baptist and other congregationally governed churches unnecessarily forgo the advanced medical attention available from that ancient spiritual hospital—the global and historic church. First Calvary gave up its power to govern itself for a little while, but that relinquishment constituted a bold and faith-infused act of self-governance. We did not scrutinize our next pastor, but we did scrutinize the scrutinizer. We did not choose our next pastor, but we did choose his chooser. So far the evidence indicates that the chooser chose well.

Chapter Eleven

ANSWERING THE DIVINE CALL

The spring of 2007 was a crazy time for me (Darrin). I had just finished a five-year run where The Journey had grown by hundreds and Acts 29 had also exploded across North America and in several other continents. My family was multiplying, and we had three kids less than seven years of age. I was also smack in the middle of doctoral work and had recently begun my dissertation. I was overwhelmed and tired. I had been diagnosed with ulcerative colitis and was having trouble sleeping through the night—which was weird because I wasn't worried about anything specific. But, as a wise mentor pointed out, I was worried about "everything in general." I didn't need another thing to worry about.

The Journey had grown beyond the leadership capacities of me, our elders, and the staff. I was breaking down physically and emotionally, and our ministry systems were breaking down structurally. Our young elders and staff were working really hard but didn't have the experience necessary to lead and govern this exploding church.

In the year before the "DeVine call," my wife and I had just had a baby, and The Journey launched our third Journey church and planted our second autonomous church. To top it all off, one of our local outreaches, "Theology at the Bottleworks," had come under fire from some Southern Baptist pastors in our state who were concerned that we were encouraging people to drink alcohol and that because they funded us, they, in turn, were encouraging people to drink alcohol. Largely because this group went public (without having conversations with us), the national media picked up the story. Calls flooded the office, asking me to make statements and give interviews. Eager to clear our name and also willing to use the media to let the community know about God's work in our church, I began to accept interviews. I appeared on MSNBC, was written about in *The New York Times*, and was asked to appear on Fox News.

I was on the way to the television station where I would appear live on Fox News when I thought of Kevin Cawley. I had met Kevin years earlier at an Acts 29 boot camp. I knew he was going to seminary and was considering church planting. I also knew through a blog that Kevin had some kind of connection to Kansas City and might be considering planting there. I was so stressed and pressed for time that I sent this text to Kevin: "Darrin Patrick requests convo." Then I just called Kevin as I was getting in the car to go to the interview in a suit that didn't quite fit.

He answered and sounded tired, which was logical because I was calling him at 6:00 a.m. Pacific Standard Time.

"Hey, man," I said. "I've only got five minutes to talk. I'm on my way to do an interview with Fox News about all this alcohol stuff with the Missouri Baptists. Can we just cut to the chase and pretend like me and you have caught up, and me tell you I know you're planting a church?"

Kevin's response was perfect, considering my antisocial call. "Brother, I haven't seen or heard from you for a year and a half. But if you're going to wake me up at six in the morning, you can say whatever you want. What do you want?"

"I know exactly what you're doing," I said, "and exactly where you want to plant, and I've got a guy in the heart of Westport who wants to give his building away, and I think you're the guy who's supposed to take it. Sorry to ruin your weekend, but we'll talk later." Then I hung up, because I'd arrived at the television studio and because I am quite rude.

Meanwhile, Kevin went to the bus stop and in his words, "rode it most the day around the city like a homeless man." He kept saying to himself, "My mom doesn't even know I want to plant in Kansas City. How does this guy know?"

Part of the reason why this call affected Kevin was because of what he and his wife had just gone through in the past few months, specifically the night before! Little did I know that Kevin had tons of friends and relationships in Kansas City who had been begging him to plant a church there. The problem was that his wife, Katie, had never been to the Midwest barbecue capital. So literally the week before my socially awkward call, Kevin and Katie had spent four days in Kansas City. He wanted her to "smell the air, touch the ground, and get a vibe for the city."

The Cawleys went more as learners than vision casters. They met with a host of characters ranging from rank angry pagans to fundamentalist pastors. Kevin listened patiently to questions and asked a few of his own in the course of these meetings: "What do you see God doing in this city? What are the needs of the city? What would it look like for a church to address those needs? Where would a church like this need to be located?"

Kevin told me later, "Every single person told us to plant a church in midtown, which is what I wanted to do anyway." This was music to his ears, because he had hung out there often during college with friends in the Westport area and loved it.

Kevin and Katie were shell-shocked. It seemed that the Lord was leading them to Kansas City. Kevin wisely grabbed his wife's hand as they flew back to Canada and said reality suggested a course of action: "'The heart is deceitful above all things.' We just came off an emotional ride fueled by sleep deprivation and a lot of intense conversation. Let's take a week to fast and pray, and let's not talk about KC at all. If God wants us to move to KC, He'll make it clear that we need to move to KC."

Kevin and Katie took that week to seek God. They went to dinner that Friday night to break their fast and stacked their hands in the middle of the table discerning that God, in fact, was calling them to uproot their lives and move to Kansas City to plant a new church. They stayed up late dreaming about what God might do. Katie, a nurse, had to force herself to sleep, because she had to be up early to go to work. Kevin heard his wife leaving for work the next morning but was totally awakened by a text on his phone that read, "Darrin Patrick requests convo."

Although shaken by the proximity of the phone call to his and his wife's decision, Kevin was quite reluctant to even consider merging his budding core team with an established church. My powers of persuasion were not working through the phone. I knew Kevin needed to see the building in all her glory and meet Mark DeVine.

So we offered to fly Kevin to St. Louis to spend some time with a pastor of church planting, Jonathan McIntosh. Jonathan was well known in church-planting circles and was Kevin's guide as the two of them planned on spending a day in St. Louis and then taking a short flight to Kansas City to explore this crazy three-way partnership.

I felt the weightiness of this trip. I knew that if Kevin was not interested in pursuing this partnership, it would not happen. As I talked to our elders about this wild idea of taking responsibility for a church across the state, the only thing that persuaded them to take this chance was the possibility that we could get a church planter to go to Kansas City.

Jonathan, who is charming and persuasive, kept Kevin up the night before the early flight to KC by telling him how great this opportunity was, how many church planters in Kevin's position would kill to have this kind of building in their target area, and how he would be crazy not to jump in with both feet. Kevin, who is impervious to hype, stated matter-of-factly, "I'm not going to take some kind of old church with a dilapidated building. That's exactly what my church-planting mentors warned me not to do. You don't merge with another church, because it will require too much sideways energy and will detract us from our vision."

The next day they were in Kansas City and standing outside of First Calvary getting ready to meet Mark DeVine. Mark told them the short version history of the church. All Kevin could think was how much money this building needed to simply not be condemned. But gradually as Mark shared his passion for the gospel, Kevin's heart began to soften. The three men knelt at the altar of the church. As Dr. DeVine prayed, Kevin sensed that this part-time pastor had been giving his life to shepherd the church in making a tough decision that would let emerging generations meet Jesus at the church. The three men were on their knees begging God would do something in that place for His glory in Kansas City again.

These men got up off their knees and then did a slightly less spiritual thing by going to eat lunch at a famous Kansas City barbecue joint. Kevin and Mark spent those two hours getting to know each other. Kevin, a former college football player, studied Mark's account of First Calvary's history like a playbook. He was very skeptical but found himself intrigued by the kingdom possibilities. Mark was impressed physically by the size of Kevin's neck, but more impressed spiritually by Kevin's discernment, courage, and proven track record of ministry. When Mark met Kris McGee, Kevin's right-hand man, he was equally impressed. Kevin and Kris weren't typical arrogant young pastors. They seemed to Mark to be humble and wise beyond their years. This was amazing because of a simple math equation: if you added up the ages of Kevin and Kris, they wouldn't even equal the average age of First Calvary members.

What persuaded Kevin and Kris to form this gospel partnership was a poignant question by Mark: "Do you think God wants this to go to waste?" Mark was speaking of the building, even pointing to it as he asked. Kevin heard Mark's voice, but heard God's voice in HD: "Don't let Mark's labors be wasted." Kevin and Kris agreed to continue the legacy of First Calvary and move their families to Kansas City to pastor and equip the people of God.

Chapter Twelve

TWO CHURCHES BECOME ONE

Once Kevin, Kris, and those of us at The Journey had committed to move forward, the new lead pastor at the newly renamed Redeemer Fellowship (formerly First Calvary) came to preach for the faithful saints at First Calvary. In the crowd that day were seventy "visitors"— many from the core group that Kevin had gathered. Kevin was amazed at the beauty of the architecture but even more amazed at the beauty of the people.

After many trips to Kansas City, Kevin, Kris, and their families made *the* move to Kansas City. Redeemer Fellowship launched in June of 2008 with around 150 people. The Journey paid for Mark to stay on for a couple of months as a consultant, helping the good people of First Calvary acclimate into their new church. Mark was ministered to more than he ministered as he observed Kevin and Kris skillfully and pastorally lead this new church. He then left to pursue a new position at Beeson Divinity School but returned to preach in April of 2009, when he discovered that six hundred people were attending in two morning worship services.

Mark wrote these words:

> The fulfillment of the wild dream took place
> through the wisdom and skill and faith and com-
> mitment of Darrin Patrick, the elders in St. Louis,
> Kevin Cawley, Kris McGee, and many others,

most with little or no prior involvement with First
Calvary Baptist Church, many in fact who had
never even heard of that congregation until it had
been transformed into Redeemer Fellowship. But
the wild dream also and first of all demanded from
the members of First Calvary a profound sacrifice
and relinquishment. We had to let go of something
that, although weak and needy, was not for that
reason any less precious to us.

God showed us that First Calvary belonged
not to us but to Him to whom we ourselves
belonged. His claim upon us and First Calvary
was both total and irrevocable. First Calvary was
in our hands, but only as in trust. First Calvary,
notwithstanding her struggles and weaknesses, yet
boasted tangible and palpably valuable assets: the
strategic property, the storied and hallowed worship space, ourselves, all God's possessions. How
best to invest what, though it be in our hands for
a brief time, was not originally or subsequently or
finally ours? How to invest what we held in trust
as stewards for the advance of the gospel? We had
to let go, sacrifice, lose our life to save it. I am so
glad we did.

Redeemer has continued to grow over the years in outreach but
also in inreach. Kris and Kevin were befriended by many of the First
Calvary members, but especially by one member.

Marie Privett had folded bulletins for decades at First Calvary and continued her old ministry in the new church. Marie had fallen and broken her hip and had gone in for surgery to repair it. Unfortunately, Marie contracted pneumonia and never got out of the hospital. A nurse called the church and informed Kris, who was associate pastor, secretary, and janitor, that Marie was dying. Kris promptly called Kevin to tell him he was going to the hospital, because "I don't think it's right for somebody to die alone."

Kevin and Kris got their toothbrushes and headed to the hospital to be with Marie as she passed to the other side. They read the book of Ephesians to Marie, which they were preaching from at the time. Ephesians, a book about what the church ought to be, was read to a faithful lady who had given the church all she had. After reading the Bible to her for a few hours, Kevin and Kris sang hymns to her. They told stories to her: "Marie, you'll never guess what happened last week …" They thanked her for her years of faithfulness to the Lord and this precious local church. In the middle of the night, Marie Privett went to be with her Savior as her two pastors prayed for her.

The two pastors went home and showered around 5:00 a.m. Around eight, a friend of Marie's and a First Calvary member left a voice mail saying, "You know, I'm sure you don't care or didn't know, but Marie Privett died last night." Kevin called her back and said, "Elaine, I absolutely know. Kris and I were there. I'm the one who told the nurse she died." Word spread like a wildfire that these two church planters weren't just about reaching the young but also about caring for the old. Of course, because that's what pastors do.

EPILOGUE

Within three months of Kevin's arrival in Kansas City, Mark and his family moved to Alabama. For Mark it was bittersweet. The move was great for his career, but it took him away from a place and a people in whom he had utterly invested himself. He looked forward to dropping in occasionally and seeing the work of God, to having confirmation that he had not labored in vain.

The messages Mark received from members and former members were not all sweetness and light. But the majority of these members echoed one of the lay leaders who said, "We were just momentarily confused into thinking we were the ones making those decisions, when it was actually God who was guiding us. God was in charge, not us." Every former member who remained after the merger could only stand stunned and amazed at the work of God right before their eyes:

> What I still don't understand is where all those people who are now attending Redeemer Fellowship today came from? ... That first Sunday was nearly

filled to capacity with young people, many of whom were single, many with young families, many newly married and pregnant. And some of those who were newly married and pregnant now have four children. And that growth has not slowed!!!!

With special pleasure, one member reflected on an idea given serious consideration by the congregation only a few years prior to Mark's arrival:

> I remember those fights—or should I say "heavy discussions"—over taking out the balconies, since they were no longer being utilized or necessary. Again, God knew what lay ahead, even though we didn't have a clue that in ten to fifteen years those balconies were going to be essential to the ministry of the church.

Some members recognized benefits born of the long, difficult journey they had taken together, never absolutely certain of the rightness of their decisions and always braced for unanticipated and unwelcome consequences once the steps of faith were taken:

> I feel going through those turbulent times just reinforces the fact that we are not the ones in charge, but God is the one in charge. I've learned to trust Him more, because He knows what is best and has our best interest at heart.

Many showed a new appreciation for trust, waiting upon God, and how God loves to hide much that He is doing from us only to give us glimpses, perhaps with dazzling clarity, but often only as we look back:

> It's only in retrospect that I see that the hand of God was in everything that happened. Your pressing of Darrin, Kevin Cawley praying for a church plant in Westport four years before he came to Calvary, our church group praying for God's intervention, and the several failed mergers that taught us patience. In my family, we had about given up hope. I am so glad we didn't.

Some two years after the replant, business took Mark back to Kansas City and into a worship service at Redeemer Fellowship. Mark pressed his way through the crush of strangers spilling out of the entrance of Redeemer Fellowship and made his way to the large reception and fellowship area just outside the still hauntingly beautiful but now filled-to-capacity sanctuary.

Out of the roomful of strangers, a familiar face emerged. An elderly woman, known for her weekly kneeling and praying at the altar of the old First Calvary before each Sunday-morning service, came toward Mark. She came with hands upraised and open in order to gently cradle his face as though caressing some fragile and precious object of deep affection. "Just look," she said as one hand gestured in a sweeping movement at the sea of worshippers. "Just look at what has happened. Just look."

As word of Mark's presence spread, former members searched out Mark and exchanged special remembrances. They mainly basked in each other's presences amid the evidence of the rightness of what they had ventured together. Amazingly, some of the children and grandchildren of former members who had opposed the merger and who had fallen away from Jesus Christ now served as active believers at Redeemer Fellowship.

One man, a longtime member of First Calvary, supporter of the merger, and member of the Vision Team, revealed that the replant altered his life:

> What I did not realize is that the change that came was not about being a lighthouse for the neighborhood, but salvation for me…. My wife and I struggled with some of Redeemer's methods and ways of doing things, but the message of the Gospel was highlighted regularly and clearly. It took me over a year to realize that the message of grace was for me. I needed it as much as Westport. I was a Christian in name only. It was works that got me to church, not grace. I needed the message to make me see God's plan for me. I may have been baptized many years ago, but only now do I see who God really is.

The risk The Journey took to assume legal responsibility for a dilapidated building and spiritual responsibility for this replant has grown our faith as a church. Several times in the past several years, our elders have recalled what God did in Kansas City that "didn't make sense on paper" to propel us to trust His timing and wisdom as we try to participate in the Great Commission. In our history, we have been able to help start seven other autonomous churches. Now armed with the experience from First Calvary/Redeemer, we are helping replant our fourth church. The Journey meets in Missouri and Illinois through six "Journey churches" and remains committed to transforming the world through the planting and replanting of local churches.

Redeemer Fellowship is almost six years old. As we said earlier in the book, in its heyday First Calvary had almost a thousand people after a hundred years of existence. Redeemer currently runs sixteen hundred people a week. They have had hundreds of new converts and have raised almost five hundred thousand dollars for church planting. They have helped support several church plants by sending people, coaching church planters, and through financial support—including New City Church five miles south of Waldo, Missouri, and Redeemer Dubai in the United Arab Emerites.

Kansas City has benefited by having a strong, local church in its core that is not content with having good worship services and creating programs that simply take care of its own members. Redeemer has adopted underresourced schools in the area, assisting with mentoring, tutoring, and in some cases programming. They have touched the artists in the community by providing free studio space and by facilitating community among them. They are in touch with the global reality of one hundred and fifty million orphans with several families adopting and supporting orphans.

Appendix A

"ROCKS THAT CRY OUT," OR BODIES AND BUILDINGS

My (Mark's) goals at First Calvary always included the church building itself. I wanted the newly replanted congregation to worship in that unique place. This desire grew out of the conviction that we were confronted, in the magnificent worship space at 39th and Baltimore, with more than mere bricks and mortar. Despite the daunting costs of addressing the deferred maintenance needs, I was sure that a simple dollars-and-cents-driven abandonment of that building would involve a loss, not only of wood and stone but much more. I want to offer a biblical and theological justification for this conviction and the desire to which it gave rise.

Nonchalance concerning the storied worship space at First Calvary displays features of an array of ancient heresies utterly incompatible with the teaching of Holy Scripture. These heresies include Marcionism, gnosticism, Manichaeanism, Arianism,

Apollinarianism, Eutychianism, and Docetism. This extraordinary list almost exhausts the truly great, definitive heresies of church history.[7] What these heresies share is this: a distinctive despising of matter, of the physical world, of the flesh. The church, confronted repeatedly with new forms of this, repeatedly found such teachings incompatible with both the goodness of God's creation and with the stunning reality of the Incarnation.

An especially striking precursor to these heresies is Platonic idealism, which became the proud inheritance not only of Western philosophy but of Western civilization. Platonic idealism conceives of a division within the universe between a physical and a metaphysical realm. The metaphysical (or "outside-the-physical") realm is characterized by divinity, eternity, spirituality, purity, and constancy—and for these reasons is the realm of reality, of true being. In sharp and inferior contrast is the physical realm, characterized by humanity, physicality, changeability, corruptibility, and mortality. Should some spark of the divine, by whatever means, come to reside, say, within a physical human being, redemption must involve the release of this spiritual spark from the prison of the physical body, say at death, and its escape from the physical realm into the metaphysical realm.

The unequivocal response of the church across time and geography to such notions has been—NO! God created the physical universe and said, "It is good." Because of humanity's rebellion, the whole universe, including its physical dimension, is cursed and exists under the wrath of God. But God is not only creator. He is also redeemer for all eternity, and He has said no to our no. God saves and redeems by taking on human flesh, not only without ceasing to be God but as a fitting exercise of divine freedom. He saves by dying and rising bodily. The good news for us, the beneficiaries of this saving work, emphatically includes the promise of bodily resurrection (1 Cor. 15). In a reflexive recoiling at any Platonic notion of a disembodied eternal state, Paul insists that we Christians do not want to "be found naked" or "unclothed" but "further clothed" (2 Cor. 5:1–5).

When the apostle John employed the term *logos* (word) in the first chapter of his gospel, he meant first to correct his audience's thinking and then instruct them in the truth. John chose this term precisely because of the technical philosophical freight it carried, which allowed him to deliver two corrective shocks to his audience: (1) "All things were made through him [the *logos*] and without him [the *logos*] was not anything made that was made" (John 1:3); and (2) "the Word [*logos*] became flesh and dwelt among us" (John 1:14).

In order to comprehend the initial reaction of John's audience, it might be best to imagine one of the four versions of Edvard Munch's famous paintings of *The Scream*. Why? Because "the *logos*" was a technical philosophical designation for "the control center" or "the mind" of the divine. The *logos* flourishes in the metaphysical realm alone. The last thing the *logos* should or would do is create a physical world, much less take on anything physical, including human flesh, both of which are asserted in John 1.

But John corrects misconception and instructs his audience in the truth. The physical generally and specifically poses no threat to deity. Furthermore, God's saving work extends beyond us sinners, and our bodies, to the entire created universe, which "waits with eager longing for the revealing of the sons of God" in hope because "the creation itself will be set free from its bondage to corruption and obtain the freedom of the glory of the children of God" (Rom. 8:18–24).

The promise of God meant to animate Christian hope is not of some ethereal, disembodied, ostensibly "spiritual" heaven, but rather a new heaven and a new earth, indeed, the new Jerusalem, a city coming down out of heaven. For Christians, there is nothing nonspiritual about the physical. As Abraham Kuyper so famously put it, "There is not one square inch of this universe about which Jesus Christ does not say, 'Mine.'"

God's claim upon all He has made is comprehensive and universal. Humanity's rebellion brings a curse upon both man and the physical world, but it did not alter God's universal claim in the slightest degree. That universal claim includes God's lordship over all time and space, all of history and geography, and all that occurs in both. The revelation of God's omnipresence bears special witness to this divine claim. Thus David eloquently expresses his discovery of the inescapability of God's presence in Psalm 139. God's presence occupies every space.

But the confession of divine omnipresence might suggest a kind of flat, undifferentiated presence of God everywhere. One might imagine that the presence of God everywhere rules out His special presence anywhere. But that would be a mistake. In fact it is precisely God's special presence in particular locations that demonstrates and confirms His presence everywhere.

God is especially present in the tabernacle. His special presence moves with the tabernacle. God is especially present with Moses on the mountain. God's special presence is closely related to His Word. God is especially present where He causes His Word to dwell. The impending giving of the Law makes the ground on which Moses stands holy. God's special presence coincides with His special speaking, and once this occurs, the location takes on permanent significance because, though He is present everywhere, He does not cause His word to dwell just everywhere. Thus the appropriateness of the urgent admonishment to seek Him "while he may be found" (Isa. 55:6). Thus Jesus's instruction to the newly healed man to go to the temple and show himself "to the priest and offer the gift that Moses commanded, for a proof to them" (Matt. 8:4).

Such New Testament recognition of special times and places is important, because some may be tempted to relegate the special sanctification of times and places to life under the old covenant. We are expected to learn this from Jesus's encounter with the Samaritan woman. She raises one of the many theological disputes that separated Jews from Samaritans—the argument about where one ought to worship—"Our fathers worshiped on this mountain [Mount Gerazim], but you [Jews] say that in Jerusalem is the place where people ought to worship." Jesus said to her, "Woman, believe me, the hour is coming when neither on this mountain nor in Jerusalem will you worship the Father.... But the hour is coming ... when the true worshipers will worship the Father in spirit and truth" (John 4:20–23).

Jesus's words "neither on this mountain nor in Jerusalem" anticipate future geopolitical events, but they don't deny the special sanctification of space in some new era when sanctity concerns only persons and not space. Rather, the transition is from a sharply localized special sanctification of a largely nonproselytizing people of God to new the age of the universalizing diaspora of witness—a proselytizing era with the tentacles of divine witness starting in Jerusalem and spreading to "the ends of the earth" (Acts 1:8). Now every space where the Word is proclaimed and received may be "made holy" as God makes His Word to dwell in many places.

Now the church, not any particular nation such as Israel or its temple, shall mark the space where God's special presence is manifest. The geographical sphere in which God's special presences occur is now expanding far beyond the confines of Palestine, but its geographical particularity continues unchanged. The particularity of God's special presence extends for the first time to the uttermost parts of the earth, bearing witness to God's omnipresence and multiplying the venues in which He causes His Word to dwell. But still not everywhere or everywhere the same, but at Antioch and at Philippi and at Rome.

Every space on earth and every building or structure dedicated to the worship of God becomes holy, which just means that it is set apart as witness to the triune God, to the Lord Jesus Christ. They bear witness that on this spot at a particular juncture in history, God raised up a people for Himself and did so by making His Word dwell, not everywhere the same, but here especially.

That this occurs does not mean every abandonment of a parcel of land or church building marks an act of unfaithfulness to the living God. After all, love lays down its very life for its friends. Certainly lands and buildings cannot be spared what might well be required of our very lives. But neither ought a gnostic disregard for the witnessing power of rocks and space imagine itself "spiritual" in any biblical sense. The treasuring and preserving of artifacts left behind by a loved one can be healthy or unhealthy. The healthy kind benefits from the witness such artifacts give to a life precious to God and still in God's hands. Healthy obedience to the Great Commission gives up whatever inhibits its witness, including bricks, mortar, and its own life. For just the same reason, such obedience holds onto whatever serves that witness. Pointing to the temple, Jesus said that not one stone would remain upon another, but He did not instruct God's people to commence with the demolition there and then!

A sadness attaches to the worshipless medieval churches dotting the landscape of Britain and Europe. But alongside the sadness, positive witness issues forth as well. The physical durability of these ancient houses of worship proclaims that once upon a time God was pleased to make His Word dwell there, and so there was raised up a people for Himself. From time to time one of these ancient worship spaces is reclaimed and revitalized by a new outbreak of the special presence of God. The actual ancient continuity of the body of Christ extended in time and space finds new witness in these spaces. That witness is enriched by its occurrence amidst the physical and spacial artifacts of previous witnesses, connecting in tangible ways contemporary believers with their spiritual siblings upon whose shoulders they stand.

Let us celebrate the new wave of church planting rising up in many places in North America—churches planted in elementary-school gyms, in the back rooms of cafés, and, as was the case in the first century, in the homes of believers. But let us not too easily abandon the salvageable old and storied houses of worship around us. In so far as we are able, let us let those rocks cry out.

Appendix B

THE OPEN BUSINESS MEETING

I (Mark) want to draw attention to the dangers posed by the "open business meeting" and suggest steps congregations can take to protect themselves from these dangers. In doing so, I am not calling for the abolition of church business meetings nor decrying congregational rule generally.

The degree of the "openness" of a business meeting is the extent to which members are encouraged to speak their minds in a meeting. In a completely open business meeting, every member present is, formally at least, free to say whatever he or she wishes at any time and free to make any motion calling for action at any time. That total openness is rare. Even the most dysfunctional Baptist churches I have encountered try to structure their business meetings in an orderly way that is incompatible with total openness. But many churches do incorporate within their structures "the opening of the floor" for motions, comments, or suggestions from any member present at the meeting. I believe we need to reconsider this sort of openness.

Ostensibly, the open business meeting establishes congregational rule. At First Calvary, a tiny minority of voting members attended and voted at monthly business meetings. This fact exposes a glaring gap between the standard Baptist defense of the open business meeting and the dynamics of actual decision making and control that too often prevails. Matters large and small are to be decided by "the church." Thus, in the open business meeting of many Baptist churches, any member in good standing of whatever age or expertise or experience or lack may bring motions to the floor and cast votes. But alas, large portions of the congregation choose not to attend such meetings.

"Well," comes the holstered and now drawn reply of the good Baptist who faithfully attends these meetings, "that's their choice. If they're not willing to attend, they ought not complain."

Fine. But take note. By tolerating minority participation at business meetings, these churches inscribe an enormous asterisk over their protestations about the necessity for "the church to decide."

What actually occurs and what is actually defended is the prerogative of those who do attend such midweek meetings to hold sway over decision making in the church. Over time, a small "lay ruling elite" tends to emerge. If true congregational leadership or rule or both is the aim, that is not what actually prevails within many Baptist churches. Instead, inadvertently, leadership and even ruling prerogatives are ceded to an elite group without consideration of giftedness or calling. This unevaluated group often exercises ironclad veto power over the positive efforts advanced from any other quarter within the congregation, including and often especially the pastor, who has been scrutinized, prayed over, and called to lead.

The irony is at once startling and tragic. For all the self-righteous blustering about congregational rule, rule by such an unelected and ill-equipped few is the order of the day in thousands of Baptist churches across the fruited plain.

So the open business meeting results in a drift into an unconsidered form of church governance. It also poses myriad dangers to the leadership at all levels. At First Calvary, the structure and atmosphere of the monthly business meeting suggested that whoever showed up brought expertise to the matters discussed. The openness of the meeting meant that any member was free to voice complaints in this public forum regarding any church or staff member. Periodically, the monthly meeting morphed into something like a public annual review of any person targeted by any member of the church. Anyone at any time could be put "in the dock" as it were, to stand scrutiny and cross-examination without warning. Untold damage to the congregation resulted from this open forum in both subtle and not-so-subtle ways.

These free-for-all meetings too easily degenerate into church-wide committee meetings at which members, regardless of expertise or involvement in the matters discussed, insert themselves into decision making and subvert or even undo the work of members who are actually elected to shape policy and initiate action in designated areas of ministry. Such frequent exposure of the work of staff, elected committee members, and other lay leaders to the whim of any disgruntled member greatly undermines the efforts of elected staff and elected laypersons and makes their recruitment and retention in vital positions of responsibility difficult.

Who would relish serving under such conditions? These nitpicky and too often humiliating scenarios wear down even the most conscientious servants of the church. Month after month, leaders and members are fair game for wildly random scrutiny. Members soon learn that the meeting may find them in the crosshairs at any time, so they had best come prepared to defend themselves.

Congregational forms of church governance and leadership have served the advance of the gospel and the nurture of healthy churches around the globe. Even today, one can find doctrinally sound, spiritually healthy, growing churches that are so governed. Nevertheless, congregational church governance, as it has devolved within many churches, cries out for a fresh rethinking. Where wise management of church business meetings is lacking, and where trust has broken down, what should be a tool in the hands of our gracious Lord all too easily mutates into a Devil's workshop.

That the average tenure for Southern Baptist pastors in one location hovers at around two years should not surprise us, but it should wake us up to systemic conditions that demoralize leaders.

Why do Baptists and other groups embrace the open meeting? Because they believe an open floor in a business session is necessary to maintain congregational rule. To deny the open floor for motions and comments may signal a lapse into some alien form of governance, such as Episcopal or Presbyterian, in which some smaller, privileged group within or even outside the congregation assumes the power to govern.

But this notion is mistaken. We need to make a distinction between governance and leadership. By *leadership* we refer to the day-to-day casting of vision, guiding of the flock, ministering to the congregation, and taking of responsibility for the congregation as a whole. The lead pastor assumes ultimate leadership responsibility in these and many other matters. By *governance* we refer to ultimate responsibility for the congregation, which includes even the lead pastor. Those who govern delegate responsibility for leadership and retain the prerogative to call or dismiss leaders.

The particular mechanisms congregations use to retain such power vary greatly. But as long as they retain the power to dismiss leaders, the church remains a congregationally ruled body of believers. The open business meeting is not essential to such governance. Many congregationally ruled churches have eliminated the open business meeting either completely or virtually.

Some have done so by first of all making a clear distinction between leading and governing and then adopting an elder-led, congregation-ruled form of governance. Such a configuration eliminates the confusion that ensues when open business meetings allow self-selected members to encroach upon leadership responsibilities they have not been asked to assume. In these challenging times when strong leadership is so crucial, Baptists would do well to take a close look at how the channels of leadership and governance are configured in their congregations. They should manage these channels in ways that actually foster advance of the gospel and edification of the body of Christ.

NOTES

1. There are a number of good books on church mergers. They include: Ed Stetzer and Mike Dodson, *Comeback Churches: How 300 Churches Turned Around and Yours Can, Too* (Nashville: B & H Publishing Group, 2007); Jim Tomberlin and Warren Bird, *Better Together: Making Church Mergers Work* (San Francisco: Jossey-Bass, 2012); Dirk Elliot, *Vital Merger: A New Church Start Approach that Joins Church Families Together* (Fun & Done Press, 2013).

2. Ed Stetzer and Mike Dodson, *Comeback Churches: How 300 Churches Turned Around and Yours Can, Too* (Nashville: B&H, 2007), x.

3. Daniel R. Sanchez, *Church Planting Movements in North America* (Fort Worth, TX: Church Starting Network, 2007), 18.

4. Alan Hirsch, *The Forgotten Ways: Reactivating the Missional Church* (Grand Rapids, MI: Brazos, 2007), 45.

5. Ed Stetzer and Mike Dodson, *Comeback Churches: How 300 Churches Turned Around and Yours Can Too* (Nashville: B & H Publishing Group, 2007).

6. National Congregations Study, quoted in "Fast Facts about American Religion," The Hartford Institute for Religion Research, http://hirr.hartsem.edu/research/fastfacts/fast_facts.html#sizecong, accessed October 14, 2013.

7. Add Ebionitism, Montanism, Pelagianism, and Donatism to this list, and you've fairly well covered the great heresies. Karl Barth insightfully contends that there are only two great heresies—Docetism and Ebionitism; all other heresies are the offspring of one of these two.

ACKNOWLEDGMENTS

I want to thank my wife and children, who have sacrificed much as I have traveled many miles to serve pastors and church planters in the last decade. It is such a joy that we get to serve God's church together.

I also want to thank the elders and leaders of The Journey, who willingly sent me to the nations for the sake of the gospel going forward through the local church.

—Darrin Patrick

ACKNOWLEDGMENTS

Thank you to Ted Yoder, Terry Megli, and Jason Lowe, who put their own jobs at risk in order to see First Calvary Baptist Church replanted. Thank you to Sheree Yoder, who not only hazarded the loss of employment for herself and her husband but also voiced a bold, heartfelt, and public plea for the replanting of First Calvary at just the right moment. Thank you to Bill and Mary Beard, whose persistent ministry to international exchange students somehow convinced me that significant and expanded ministry could happen at First Calvary.

Thank you to vision team members Barbara Mcklin, Robert Revels, and the late Lynn Gregg, who, sometimes against their own instincts, trusted me, gave me the benefit of the doubt, and supported me against significant opposition. Special thanks to Steve Turley and Elaine Russell, who not only provided wise council but acted as strategic bridges of communication between opposing factions over many months of difficult struggle.

Very special thanks to Jim Overman, whose wisdom, steadiness, confidence in me, and faith in the providence of God saved me from despair more times than he knows. Thank you to the deacons of First Calvary Baptist Church, who embraced their sobering responsibilities during these years with unusual courage and self-sacrifice. Thanks to former pastor Fred Fishel, who offered personal support and encouragement to me at more than one low point in the long saga of change at First Calvary and challenged the congregation to put the advance of the gospel above personal preference as we faced momentous decisions together. Thank you to the many members on all sides of the shared struggle who invested their lives at real cost to themselves in myriad ways because they wanted to see the name of Jesus Christ honored in their midst.

Finally, thanks to my coauthor, Darrin Patrick, and to the founding lead pastor of Redeemer Fellowship, Kevin Cawley, both of whom embraced the unique and formidable challenges presented by the replanting of First Calvary Baptist Church.

—Mark DeVine

ABOUT THE AUTHOR

Darrin Patrick founded The Journey in 2002 in the urban core of St. Louis, Missouri. The Journey has six locations and has released seven church plants. Darrin is vice president of the Acts 29 Church Planting Network and has helped start multiple nonprofits in St. Louis. He also serves as chaplain to the St. Louis Cardinals. Darrin's passion is to help people know and live in the gospel.

After earning his BA in biblical languages from Southwest Baptist University and a Master of Divinity (summa cum laude) from Midwestern Baptist Theological Seminary, Darrin earned his Doctor of Ministry from Covenant Seminary. Darrin's first book, *Church Planter: The Man, the Message, the Mission*, with Crossway, was released in 2010. Darrin's second book, *For the City*, with Zondervan, was released in 2011. His new book, *The Dude's Guide to Manhood*, with Thomas Nelson, was released in

2014. Darrin is married to his high-school sweetheart, Amie, and they have four beautiful children: Glory, Grace, Drew, and Delainey.

Find out more about Darrin Patrick at:

Blog/Resources – www.DarrinPatrick.org
Twitter - @DarrinPatrick
Facebook.com/DarrinPatrick

ABOUT THE COAUTHOR

 Mark DeVine serves as associate professor of divinity at the Beeson Divinity School of Samford University in Birmingham, Alabama. Dr. DeVine is the author of numerous articles, book chapter contributions, and *Bonhoeffer Speaks Today: Following Jesus at All Costs*, published by LifeWay. DeVine served as a missionary to Bangkok, Thailand; has pastored churches in Kentucky, Indiana, Missouri, and South Carolina; and frequently serves as an interim pastor. He lives in Hoover, Alabama, with his wife, Jackie. They are the parents of two grown sons.

WHY ACTS 29?

www.Acts29Network.org

BY MATT ADAIR

In the summer of 2004, I became the pastor of Christ Church Presbyterian, a church of fewer than one hundred people just outside of Athens, Georga. The church had gone through a hard breakup with the founding pastor, and I was twenty-eight and too young to know how dumb I was. Neither of us should have made it.

Now here we are, months away from my tenth anniversary as lead pastor of what is now known as Christ Community Church. The church has been better to me than I've been to the church. A pastor's first church is the equivalent of a sixteen-year-old's first car—you're bound to rag the thing out. But God has been kind and kept us together. I've never enjoyed our church more and am grateful that we've been able to follow Jesus together.

By all accounts, we are not an evangelical success story. We number in the hundreds, not the thousands. We are not theological enough for some; we are not evangelistic enough for others; we are not established enough for families; and we are not trendy enough for hipsters.

We are stunningly, overwhelmingly ordinary.

One of the reasons that I've been able to embrace our ordinariness is the Acts 29 Church Planting Network. Our church became a covenant member of Acts 29 in 2007, and I have served as the director of operations for the entire network since 2013. And while there are well-known pastors and extraordinary churches in Acts 29, we are primarily a network of ordinary men leading ordinary churches.

And it is in the ordinariness that many of us find our hope—the thrill that an extraordinary God would call men like us such an extraordinary work. There is an odd blueprint that produces church planters and replanters. Humble entrepreneurs. Hard workers who prioritize their families. Historic theology applied to an ever-changing context. Ordinary men doing extraordinary work in five hundred churches around the world, in twenty-four countries, spread across six continents. The men who lead Acts 29 churches are men who don't make the grade in the eyes of the world. Wasted ambition. Curators of an archaic way of life.

But make no mistake, there is a blueprint. Spiritual vitality. Theological clarity. Emotional maturity. Entrepreneurial ability. A follower of Jesus, a family man, and a friend to the people God has placed around him. There are as many ways to advance the kingdom of God as there are ways to score touchdowns in the Super Bowl.

This is our way.

If you are considering the work of replanting, we would love to help you. If you have already replanted a church and want your church to plant or replant other churches, let's talk. Email me directly at mca@acts29network.org, and mention this book.

Matt Adair is the director of operations
for the Acts 29 Network and the lead
pastor of Christ Community Church in
Athens, Georgia (missionathens.com).

*For more information about the Acts 29 Church
Planting Network, go to www.Acts29Network.org/About*